The Thanksgiving Book

An Illustrated Treasury of Lore, Tales, Poems, Prayers, and the Best in Holiday Feasting

Introduction by Willard Scott

Created by Jerome Agel and Jason Shulman
Edited by Melinda Corey

A Blue Cliff Editions Book
A Dell Trade Paperback

"Old Sturbridge Village Roast Turkey with Lemon and Ham Stuffing Balls," "Mulled Cider," and "Sweet Taters and Apples" from *Recipes from America's Restored Villages* by Jean Anderson. Copyright © 1975 by Jean Anderson. Reprinted by permission of Doubleday & Company, Inc.

"Prayer/Aztec" and "Prayer/Iroquois" from *In the Trail of the Wind* edited by John Bierhorst. Copyright © 1971 by John Bierhorst. Reprinted by permission of Farrar, Straus and Giroux, Inc.

"Leftovers" from *It's Thanksgiving* by Jack Prelutsky. Text: Copyright © 1982 by Jack Prelutsky. By permission of Greenwillow Books (A Division of William Morrow).

"Prayer to the Corn Mothers"/Tewa and "Prayer Before Eating"/Arapaho from *The Sacred Path* edited by John Bierhorst. Text: Copyright © 1983 by John Bierhorst. By permission of William Morrow & Company.

Grandma's Kitchen, "Grandma Hepford's Oyster Stuffing," "Grandma Hepford's Chestnut Stuffing," "Grandmother Galatha Sterner's Thanksgiving Mustard Onions," "Grandma Conner's Baking Powder Biscuits," "Myrtle Orloff's Appleanna Bread," "Mama Boyd's Sweet-Potato Pie," Copyright © 1985 by Blue Cliff Editions, Inc. Reprinted by permission of Simon & Schuster, Inc.

Madge Lorwin, "White Ipocras" and "Furmenty" from *Dining with William Shakespeare*. Copyright © 1976 Madge Lorwin. Reprinted with the permission of Atheneum Publishers.

"Chinese Turkey Salad," "Garden-Patch Turkey Stew with Dumplings," and "Turkey Barley Chowder" reprinted by permission of Butterball Turkey/Swift-Eckrich, Inc. 1987. "Healthy Hints" and "Comparison of Roasting Methods and Special Tips" adapted with permission of Butterball Turkey/Swift-Eckrich, Inc. 1987.

A Dell Trade Paperback
Published by
Dell Publishing
a division of
The Bantam Doubleday Dell Publishing Group, Inc.
666 Fifth Avenue
New York, New York 10103

Book design by Nina Clayton

The trademark Dell® is registered in the U.S. Patent and Trademark Office.
ISBN: 0-440-58503-1

Printed in the United States of America

November 1987
10 9 8 7 6
MV

Acknowledgments

This book would not exist without the contributions of many helpful and knowledgeable people and organizations. We gratefully acknowledge the following for granting permission to publish their recipes:
- James Baker, Plimouth Plantation
- Rick Accola, Gravymaster, Inc.
- Susan Q. Bruno, The Colonial Williamsburg Foundation

We would also like to thank:
- Willard Scott and Nancy Field
- Mary Davis, the Museum of the American Indian
- Gene Smith and Mary C. Kennamer, the National Wild Turkey Federation
- Kristi Kienholz, Old Sturbridge Village
- Culver Pictures and the New York Public Library Picture Collection
- Peter Pickow, for song arrangements, and Amy Appleby, for editorial and picture research
- Jackie Ogburn and Julie Polkes, for countless editorial suggestions and much support

Contents

Over My River and Through My Wood: Why I Love Thanksgiving

WILLARD SCOTT

"Hurrah for the fun! Is the turkey done?
Hurrah for the pumpkin pie!"
—Lydia Maria Child, "Over the River and Through the Wood"

"Thanksgiving Day Arrival at the Old Home," nearly two hundred years ago (Culver Pictures)

Over My River and Through My Wood: Why I Love Thanksgiving

WILLARD SCOTT

Over the years, I have had the glorious opportunity to visit nearly every state in the Union, and I never fail to be astounded by our country's variety of people and places. I can step out of a bustling subway and into a breathtaking performance at New York's glittering Lincoln Center, tool around a Michigan blueberry farm, dig for clams along a deserted beach in Maine, or join in foot-stomping fun at Nashville's Grand Ole Opry. These adventures are all very different, but together they represent the fabric of this land I love.

One of the strongest similarities I have found in all of us Americans is the way we treat holidays. We all love holidays: they give us a reason to abandon routine, to celebrate, and to make memories. What holiday gives us a better chance to do all these things than Thanksgiving? Thanksgiving weekend is for most of us the longest, least interrupted weekend of the year. It is the ideal time for family and friends to come together again. It is also the most purely American of all holidays, because it celebrates the settling of our country by the Pilgrims over 350 years ago.

For me, Thanksgiving conjures up all the things in life that I respond to most strongly and for which I am truly grateful. There is the simple beauty of the earth and the blessed bounty shared at harvest time. There is the satisfaction that comes from working a crop, the wisdom that comes from knowing that if you handle the land with care, it will yield a rich reward. And there is the tradition of the day itself: the return to my family homesteads in the green hills of Maryland and Virginia, the mouthwatering food, and of course the sharing in the holiday rituals.

My father tells me that I spent my first Thanksgiving sprawled on the parlor floor of our family friend Mrs. Tyree's home while happily clutching a roasted turkey leg. But my earliest Thanksgiving memories come from my grandparents' old farm a few years later. For as long as I can remember, my grandparents have had a 75-acre farm in the happily named town of Freeland, in the rolling hills of Harford County, Maryland. Although I visit it now only much too infrequently, it was once the center of my life. The farmhouse was an anchor for the family during the dark days of the Second World War. The garden and the chicken coop fed us well. Everyone knows that good food and sentiments of the heart are closely linked. I learned about that union early on—under the apple trees, in the middle of the tomato patch, and especially in my grandfather's smokehouse. The smokehouse was his pride and joy. It was always clean as a whistle and rich with the pungent smells of freshly cured meats. I got my first lessons in dry curing meats the Southern way from my grandfather Scott. When I bought my own farm in Virginia a few years ago, I built a smokehouse for myself!

With food in such abundance and held in such high regard in the Scott household, you can imagine the role the holiday meal played on the farm in Freeland. Nothing evoked the spirit of the holiday like a resounding dinner. It aroused healthy conversation, mended family fences, and made any reason to celebrate doubly special.

I was five years old when I spent my first Thanksgiving at the farm. The year 1939 was historic for many reasons, but for the Scotts it was especially memorable—it was the first time in years we celebrated a wedding in the farmhouse, and it was the only time the house almost became the site of the honeymoon, too! I still remember helping to haul my Aunt Mabel and her new husband to the train station in the middle of an unseasonal snowstorm. Grandfather Scott had planned to rev up his shiny black Dodge and drive the newlyweds to the local train station after dinner, but the moment we bit into our first slice of turkey it started to snow: big wet flakes with lots of sticking power and a wind strong enough to make the snow dance and render windshield wipers useless. "Don't worry," my grandfather said, and we finished the meal. In minutes, everything went— the huge roast turkey, the cooling cranberry sauce, the heavenly clouds of just-whipped potatoes, and our family heirloom pies—the creamy, tangy pumpkin and the deep-dish apple, fragrant with cinnamon and nutmeg. After dinner, my father and grandfather raced to the barn and hitched the two dapple grays to the sleigh. We had a ride I've never forgotten—the entire Scott family and the anxious newlyweds dashing through the snow in a two-horse open sleigh to catch the Honeymoon Express!

When we returned to the house, we retired to the parlor, cranked up the Victrola, and chimed in with the dulcet tones of Nat Shilkret's orchestra—"singing for our supper," we called it. To this day, we sing for our supper in the Scott household, but now, in addition to the family favorites, we sing the standards from our hymnals—"We Gather Together," "Onward, Christian Soldiers," and "Amazing Grace."

In the Scott household, the Thanksgiving traditions have never waned, they've just changed a bit. Although I now live in Manhattan, I never spend

Thanksgiving away from a farm. Instead of my grandparents', it is now my own homestead in Middleburg, Virginia. Both my wife and I love to cook, and we try to be extra-imaginative on the holidays. In addition to the family favorites, we've added to our repertoire a dandy tomato aspic, a sinfully rich sweet potato casserole, and a heavenly coconut and mandarin orange salad. But no matter how the menu changes, no matter whether we are serving roast goose instead of turkey or Southern pecan pie instead of apple, the sentiment remains the same. The spirit of the Thanksgiving holiday promotes life, letting friendship, closeness, and unity bloom. Everyone who shares a Thanksgiving meal with us becomes a friend, and every friend an honorary member of the family.

I like to believe that I can remember clearly every taste, every smell, every slightly off-key note from our player piano—everything except where all the Thanksgivings went. As I grow older, the celebrations seem to merge into one grand set of the best memories. I'll always remember Thanksgivings as the times we ate good food, sang old-fashioned songs, and shared a lot of love with our family and friends. May your Thanksgivings bring you the same kind of joy.

A BRIEF HISTORY OF THANKSGIVING IN AMERICA

"Our harvest being gotten in, our Governor sent four men on fowling, so that we might after a special manner rejoice together after we had gathered the fruit of our labor. They four in one day killed as much fowl as, with a little help beside, served the company almost a week. At which time, amongst other recreations, we exercised our arms, many of the Indians coming among us, and among the rest their greatest King Massasoit, with some ninety men, whom for three days we entertained and feasted . . . ."

—Edward Winslow, one of the Pilgrim Fathers recalling the Plymouth celebration of 1621

"The First Thanksgiving, New Plymouth, 1621," by W.L. Sheppard (Culver Pictures)

From the Pilgrims' feasts with the Indians at Plymouth to celebrations back home with family and friends, from bountiful tables laden with roast turkey, cranberry sauce, and pumpkin pie to the ritual of watching Thanksgiving Day parades, we all have our images of Thanksgiving. It is a holiday that blends the familiar, the festive, and the religious in a truly American mix. But the Thanksgiving we enjoy today is vastly different from the Thanksgivings celebrated a few generations ago, and even further from the Thanksgivings celebrated over three centuries ago.

When was the first Thanksgiving? To find the origins of this holiday, we must look beyond the founding of our country and back to the first festivals that celebrated the bounty of the earth and the rewards of the year's harvest.

Harvest home festivals, celebrations to the gods in thanks for the harvest, are found in almost every culture. In biblical times, the Hebrews held the Feast of Tabernacles; the ancient Greeks held festivals in honor of Demeter, the goddess of harvests; the Romans held a celebration called the Cerealia, in honor of Ceres, the goddess of grain. When European settlers came to the New World in the early 1600s, a number of religious and harvest festivals were still being celebrated on the continent, and all of them lay the groundwork for Thanksgiving as we know it today.

By far the best known of the first Thanksgiving harvest ceremonies here is the three-day feast celebrated in the fall of 1621 by English settlers at Plymouth, Massachusetts.

A year earlier, in the winter of 1620, 102 English colonists had landed in southeastern Massachusetts. The area had been explored by English Captain John Smith (of Pocahontas fame) in 1614, and the waters there, rich with a variety of fish, had been harvested by the English since the early 1500s.

The Plymouth settlers were in search of a new home. Several of them were refugees, known as Separatists, who had rebelled against the rites and discipline of the Church of England. They believed that the Church had not done enough to reform itself since Henry VIII had divided the Church of England from the Catholic Church in 1534. In 1607, the Separatists emigrated to Holland to establish a new religious community. Their settlement in Holland lasted for twelve years. The group then uprooted itself and some sailed west for the New World.

The Pilgrims, aboard the *Mayflower*, landed at Plymouth in December 1620. Their supplies were depleted by the voyage, and they could not plant crops because it was winter. Many of the group died. By the spring, only

55 of the original 102 settlers were still alive. It was only with the assistance of the Wampanoag Indians that the colonists survived. Tisquantum, also known as Squanto, one of the first Indians to make peace with the settlers, showed them how to plant corn and squash and how to hunt and fish in the unfamiliar territory.

In the autumn of 1621, the settlers harvested their first crops. If it were not for these native American staples, the Pilgrims would have starved to death: none of the seeds brought aboard the *Mayflower*—with the exception of barley—yielded usable crops.

To celebrate the bounty, Governor William Bradford proclaimed a three-day feast and celebration, and invited the Indians to join in the festivities. This is the feast that is known to most of us as the first Thanksgiving in America. It was a joyful occasion, featuring games, displays of arms, a bounteous table, and a unity between the Native Americans and the English settlers. In one of the only firsthand accounts of the feast, Edward Winslow, one of the Pilgrim Fathers, wrote:

> Our harvest being gotten in, our Governor sent four men on fowl-ing, so that we might after a special manner rejoice together after we had gathered the fruit of our labor. They four in one day killed as much fowl as, with a little help beside, served the company almost a week. At which time, amongst other recreations, we exercised our arms, many of the Indians coming among us, and among the rest their greatest King Massasoit, with some ninety men, whom for three days we entertained and feasted, and they went out and killed five deer, which they brought to the plantation and bestowed on our governor, and upon the captain, and others.

Other early Thanksgiving celebrations included a prayer service that took place in Jamestown, Virginia, in 1619 and a celebration in the Massachusetts Bay Colony in 1630. While these celebrations were offerings of thanksgiving, they did not lead to the declaration of an annual holiday.

Over the decades that followed, days of thanksgiving became more frequent in Puritan New England, and debate about making the celebration a civil holiday grew. Many later colonists believed in the strict division of secular and ecclesiastical powers, that authority to declare days of thanksgiving should lie with the church, not with the state. But gradually, the boundary between religious and civil services grew less strict, and by the eighteenth century the governors of Connecticut, Massachusetts, and New Hampshire were proclaiming an autumn Thanksgiving celebration of prayer and feasting.

During the American Revolution, days of public thanksgiving focused on the goals and successes of the Continental Army, thus following the tradi-

THE INDIANS
AND THE PILGRIMS

In a history that was epitomized by conflict, Thanksgiving commemorates a time of great cooperation between the Indians and the Pilgrims. In fact, on the first Thanksgiving Day, the Pilgrims celebrated their friendship with the Native Americans and offered their thanks to God for helping them survive the deadly winter of 1620–1621.

The Wampanoag (also known as the Pokanoket) was the Native American tribe that lived in the region where the Pilgrims landed. At the time the Pilgrims arrived, the tribe was under enormous pressure: nearly three-fourths of its number had been killed by diseases introduced by foreign explorers, and the remaining members were fending off attacks from a neighboring tribe, the Narragansett.

The Pilgrims were also confronting the crisis of survival. Almost half of the new settlers had died of scurvy, caused by poor nutrition, or of exposure, caused by the lack of adequate shelter. With both the Indians and the newcomers struggling to stay alive, the time was ripe for a friendship that could benefit each side.

The first contact between the two groups was made by Samoset and Squanto, Indians who, after being kidnapped and enslaved by English traders, had escaped their captors on a return voyage to America. Because Samoset, an Abnaki Indian from Maine, and Squanto, a Wampanoag, both now spoke English, they were able to arrange a meeting between Massasoit, the chief of the Wampanoag, and the first governor of Plymouth Colony, John Carver. The treaty of mutual support they negotiated said in part:

1. That neither he nor any of his
cont. on p. 9

tion of proclaiming holidays to honor important public causes and events. The defeat of British General John Burgoyne at Saratoga, which marked a turning point in the Revolutionary War prompted the first *national* day of thanksgiving. On December 18, 1777, the Continental Congress proclaimed a "day of solemn Thanksgiving and praise" for that "signal success." In the years following the British surrender at Yorktown in October 1781, Congress routinely proclaimed a number of days of thanksgiving to hail the survival of the United States of America.

"Mankind is never truly thankful for the benefits of life until they have experienced the want of them."
—An Army surgeon near Valley Forge,
on the first official national
Thanksgiving Day, 1789

By the late 1840s, Thanksgivings were celebrated in Connecticut, Massachusetts, New Hampshire, Rhode Island, Vermont, Maine, New York, Michigan, Illinois, Iowa, Wisconsin, Indiana, Missouri, and Pennsylvania. Each put its stamp on the holiday, but all celebrated with huge feasts. As settlers moved west, Thanksgiving homecomings to the East became common. Festive evening events, such as parlor games and dances, were popular.

It is generally acknowledged that Sarah Josepha Hale, editor of the influential magazine *Godey's Lady's Book*, was the central force in making

Thanksgiving an annual national holiday. In 1846, Mrs. Hale began her drive to establish the last Thursday in November as Thanksgiving Day. She devoted each November issue of her magazine to the idea. She wrote editorials urging the holiday and features on how to celebrate it properly. In the early 1860s, she wrote letters to the governor of every state and territory, requesting that a national Thanksgiving Day be proclaimed. She now saw Thanksgiving as a way to promote a spirit of national unity in a country divided by civil war.

In 1863, President Abraham Lincoln announced not one, but two national days of thanksgiving. The first, in August, celebrated the victory of the Union Army at Vicksburg, which Mr. Lincoln hoped would be a return to peace:

> I do set apart Thursday, the 6th day of August next, to be observed as a day of national thanksgiving, praise, and prayer, . . . (to) render the homage due to the Divine Majesty for the wonderful things he has done in the nation's behalf, and . . . to subdue the anger which has produced and so long sustained a needless and cruel rebellion . . . and finally to lead the whole nation through the paths of repentance and submission to the Divine Will back to the perfect enjoyment of union and fraternal peace.

This was not enough for Mrs. Hale. In September, she asked the

cont. from p. 8

    should injure or do hurt to any of their people.

2. That if any of his did hurt any of theirs, he should send the offender, that they might punish him.
3. That if anything were taken away from any of theirs, he should cause it to be restored; and they should do the like to his.
4. If any did unjustly war against him, they would aid him; if any did war against them, he should aid them.
5. He should send to his neighbours confederates to certify them of this, that they might not wrong them, but might be likewise compromised in the conditions of peace.
6. That when their men came to them, they should leave their bows and arrows behind them.

During the next few months, the Native Americans and the settlers worked together to till the land and plant the first successful crops. The first feast of Thanksgiving, in October of 1621, was a harvest festival filled with fellowship, good food, and games. The Indians and the colonists shared the fruits of their labor: venison, duck, turkey, corn, and pumpkin.

The peace born of mutual support and trust eventually eroded. In 1675, a full-scale war erupted between the descendants of the Pilgrims and the Indians. Now known as King Philip's War, after the English name for Chief Massasoit's son, who was now the chief, the clash lasted eleven years and caused great destruction to both sides. The Wampanoag was defeated, and peaceful relations between the two groups were forever shattered.

THE FIRST PRESIDENTIAL THANKSGIVING PROCLAMATION

George Washington declared the first official national Thanksgiving Day, in 1789, in his first year as president. In his proclamation, he cited the nationwide peace and the ratification of the Constitution:

I do recommend and assign Thursday, the twenty-sixth of November next, to be devoted by the people of these states to the service of that great and glorious Being; . . . for the signal and manifold mercies, and the favorable interpositions of his providence in the course and conclusion of the late war; for the great degree of tranquility, union, and plenty, which we have since enjoyed; for the peaceable and rational manner in which we have been enabled to establish Constitutions of Government for our safety and happiness. . . .

Over the next few decades, only Presidents John Adams and James Madison proclaimed national Thanksgiving celebrations. The other presidents left the decision about a Thanksgiving Day to the governors of each state, leaving the presidency out of the still active debate over the right of a civil government to proclaim a national religious holiday.

"May we ask guidance in more surely learning the ancient truth that greed and selfishness and striving for undue riches can never bring lasting happiness or good."
—President Franklin Delano Roosevelt, 1933

president "to have the *day of our annual Thanksgiving made a national and fixed Union Festival.*" On October 3, Mr. Lincoln proclaimed an annual nationwide Thanksgiving Day. It was to be celebrated on the last Thursday of November. It would be a day of "Thankgiving and praise to our beneficent Father who dwelleth in the heavens." Over 200 years in the making, this national Thanksgiving brought together all the elements of the past Thanksgivings: the harvest festival, national patriotism, and civil and religious observances.

Thanksgiving had at last become a national institution. Parades became common, having grown from the simple displays of arms at the Plymouth Thanksgiving to elaborate processions and rituals, especially of firemen and the military. In 1921, Gimbel's in Philadelphia inaugurated the department store-sponsored Thanksgiving Day parade. The annual Macy's Thanksgiving Day Parade was started in New York in 1924; today, it is one of the best known traditions of the holiday.

During the late 1860s and in the 1870s, local baseball games had dominated Thanksgiving holiday afternoons. But by the 1880s, football had become the national Thanksgiving sport. College games predominated, the star attraction being Yale vs. Harvard at the Polo Grounds in New York City. In 1934, the Detroit Lions established the tradition of a professional football game on Thanksgiving

Day itself, broadcast first on radio, today on television.

The First World War brought a change in the celebration. Grain, meat, and sugar needed for the troops were scrupulously avoided by homemakers. The Depression brought the greatest change in Thanksgiving in this century. In 1939, President Franklin Delano Roosevelt changed the date of the holiday. To hasten the nation's economic recovery from the Depression, he announced that the date of Thanksgiving would be moved to a week earlier in the month, expanding the Christmas buying season. This stirred the nation to debate. A ten-year-old addressed the problem succinctly in her letter to the president: "I will be very angry if you change Thanksgiving, because for one reason, the Pilgrims started it and if it hadn't [been] for the Pilgrims North America wouldn't be here and you probably wouldn't be our President today. The other reason is, it sometimes comes on my birthday. . . ."

On May 20, 1941, President Roosevelt announced that Thanksgiving would return to its original date. Members of Congress introduced bills to fix the date permanently. On December 26, 1941, Public Law #379 established the fourth Thursday in November as the official date of the national holiday of Thanksgiving. It is to this day the date of America's own movable feast.

THANKSGIVING IN CANADA

Thanksgiving Day in Canada is the second Monday in October. There are no parades, no football games, no shopping mall displays. The holiday is seen simply as a time for families and friends to share a meal and, according to the 1957 proclamation from Ottawa, to thank "Almighty God for the blessings with which the people of Canada have been favored." Like the American holiday, the Canadian Thanksgiving has its roots in harvest home festivals and civil days of public thanksgiving, but it is without the links to the country's founding that make the celebration so important in the United States.

The earliest Canadian Thanksgivings were, like the days of thanksgiving during the American Revolution, celebrations declared to mark successes in important battles. In 1760, for instance, the town of Halifax, Nova Scotia, proclaimed a Thanksgiving observance to hail the English victory over the French at Montreal during the Seven Years' War. The first official Canadian Thanksgiving was not proclaimed until 1871. It celebrated the return to health of the Prince of Wales in "Mother England." The annual Thanksgiving holiday to reflect on the blessings of the land was first proclaimed in 1879.

Dates for celebrating the holiday varied from province to province, falling anywhere between the first week of October and the second week of November. This practice continued until 1957, when the government set the official date as the second Monday in October. The date was close to harvesting time and was thus more in keeping with the tradition of giving thanks for the earth's bounty.

THANKSGIVING PSALMS AND PRAYERS

*"Let us come before his presence with
thanksgiving; and show ourselves glad in him
with psalms."*

—*The Book of Common Prayer*

"Thanksgiving Day, November 26, 1863," by Thomas Nast
(Picture collection, the Branch Libraries,
the New York Public Library)

O ur earliest Thanksgivings centered on religious services. A typical Thanksgiving in New England in the late 1600s included two lengthy church services, one in the morning and one in the afternoon, with dinner in between. At these services, prayers and psalms were both spoken and sung. Today, even though feasting and celebration have become more associated with the holiday, Thanksgiving prayers and psalms—now sometimes with music added—remain an active element.

No selection of prayers for Thanksgiving would be appropriate without prayers by Native Americans, who made the first Thanksgiving possible. Some of the prayers here are even older than Thanksgiving itself: the ''Aztec Prayer'' originated in the 1500s. Others, like ''Prayer Before Eating'' of the Arapaho Indians, of Minnesota, Wyoming, and Colorado, date well after the first Thanksgiving of the Pilgrims, and undoubtedly were influenced by the Christian teachings of the Europeans. While the Native Americans did not have a fixed Thanksgiving holiday, their prayers are included to give you the flavor of the Indians' close relationship to the earth and its harvest, which, after all, was what the Pilgrim settlers were thankful for.

Bring back an old Thanksgiving ritual this year. Start your meal with the joyful noise of ''thanksgiving.''

''It is a good thing to give thanks unto the Lord.''
—Psalm 106:1

Psalm 100

Make a joyful noise to the
Lord, all the lands!
Serve the Lord with gladness!
Come into his presence with singing!

Know that the Lord is God!
It is he that made us, and we are his;
we are his people, and the sheep of his pasture.

Enter his gates with thanksgiving,
and his courts with praise!
Give thanks to him, bless his name!

For the Lord is good;
his steadfast love endures for ever,
and his faithfulness to all generations.

Psalm 111

Praise the Lord.
I will give thanks to the Lord with my whole heart,
in the company of the upright, in the congregation.
Great are the works of the Lord,
studied by all who have pleasure in them.
Full of honor and majesty is his work,
and his righteousness endures for ever.
He has caused his wonderful works to be remembered;
the Lord is gracious and merciful.
He provides food for those who fear him;
he is ever mindful of his covenant.
He has shown his people the power of his works,

in giving them the heritage of the nations.
The works of his hands are faithful and just;
all his precepts are trustworthy,
they are established for ever and ever,
to be performed with faithfulness and uprightness.
He sent redemption to his people;
he has commanded his covenant for ever.
Holy and terrible is his name!
The fear of the Lord is the beginning of wisdom;
a good understanding have all those who practice it.
His praise endures for ever!

Aztec Prayer

Lord most giving and resourceful,
I implore you;
make it your will
that this people enjoy
the goods and riches you naturally give,
that naturally issue from you,
that are pleasing and savory,
that delight and comfort,
though lasting but briefly,
passing away as if in a dream.
—*Circa 1500s*

"Gratitude is the sign of noble souls."
—Aesop

Tewa Prayer to the Corn Mothers

Our old women gods, we ask you!
Our old women gods, we ask you!
Then give us long life together,
May we live until our frosted hair
Is white; may we live till then
This life that now we know!

—Traditional

Iroquois Prayer

We return thanks to our mother, the earth, which sustains us. We return thanks to the rivers and streams, which supply us with water. We return thanks to all herbs, which furnish medicines for the cure of our diseases. We return thanks to the corn, and to her sisters, the beans and squash, which give us life. We return thanks to the bushes and trees, which provide us with fruit. We return thanks to the wind, which, moving the air, has banished diseases. We return thanks to the moon and stars, which have given to us their light when the sun was gone. We return thanks to our grandfather *He-no,* that he has protected his grandchildren from witches and reptiles, and has given to us his rain. We return thanks to the sun, that he has looked upon the earth with a beneficent eye. Lastly, we return thanks to the Great Spirit, in whom is embodied all goodness, and who directs all things for the good of his children.

—*Circa 1800s*

Arapaho Prayer Before Eating

Our father, hear us, and our grandfather. I mention also
all those that shine, the yellow day, the good wind,
the good timber, and the good earth.

All the animals, listen to me under the ground. Animals
above ground, and water animals, listen to me. We
shall eat your remnants of food. Let them be good.

Let there be long breath and life. Let the people
increase, the children of all ages, the girls and the
boys, and the men of all ages and the women, the
old men of all ages and the old women. The food
will give us strength whenever the sun runs.

Listen to us, Father, Grandfather. We ask thought,
heart, love, happiness. We are going to eat.

—Traditional

*"A thankful heart is not only the greatest virtue, but the
parent of all other virtues."*
—Cicero

THE THANKSGIVING FEAST

"Come home to Thanksgiving!
Dear children, come home!
From the Northland and the South,
from West and the East,
Where'er ye are resting, where'er ye roam,
Come back to this sacred
and annual feast."

—Horace Greeley, editor and political leader,
"To All New Englanders," 1846

"Preparing for Thanksgiving," 1873, artist unknown (Culver Pictures)

F irst comes the aroma of the turkey roasting, then the smell of the favorite family sweet potato casserole cooking in the oven. Someone places the pumpkin pies on the kitchen window ledge to cool. In a large bowl, waiting to be mixed, are the ingredients for Grandma Hepford's Chestnut Stuffing—freshly blanched chestnuts, sweet butter, and just-grated bread crumbs. Presently, the gleaming table will be ready. One by one, family and friends take their seat at the feast.

Everyone has a favorite Thanksgiving specialty. For some, it is a hearty stuffing from a recipe that has been passed down for generations. For others, it is a fabulous pecan tart tasted first at a historical country inn. Almost everyone seems to know ''the absolutely best way'' to cook a turkey, and those who don't, know the best way to eat it.

In the following pages is the ultimate Thanksgiving feast, composed of the very best recipes the holiday offers. This culinary odyssey will take you across America and Canada for the finest in holiday feasting, from side dish to stuffing. There are recipes from the best country inns in Vermont and Minnesota, and historical recipes you can make, so you may experience food the way the earliest settlers prepared it during their celebrations. You'll also delight in the holiday home-cooking specialties collected from grandmothers from all over the country. The women who created these recipes are not national celebrity chefs; they are simply home cooks who knew how to prepare food well and whose native inspiration helped to create our quintessentially American cuisine. We hope you will make these recipes your own, and add your family traditions so that your family and friends can enjoy the most delicious in Thanksgiving eating.

(Picture collection, the
Branch Libraries, the New
York Public Library)

A Cornucopia of Thanksgiving Recipes

Soups and Appetizers

Country Corn Chowder

This house specialty from the Inn of the Golden Ox, in Brewster, Massachusetts, features one of the foods present at that first, 1621 Thanksgiving.

½ lb bacon or fatback, diced
1 large Spanish onion, diced
1 cup celery, diced
½ cup flour
2 qt chicken stock, chilled
2 cups raw potatoes, diced
½ tsp thyme
1 bay leaf
½ tsp marjoram

4 sprigs parsley
6 peppercorns, crushed
1 clove garlic
6 ears sweet corn
2 cups half-and-half or light cream
salt to taste
white pepper to taste
unsalted butter

In a 4-quart stockpot, sauté bacon or fatback until fat is rendered. With a slotted spoon remove bacon or fatback and discard, leaving fat in the stockpot. Add onion and celery, and sauté until transparent. Do not brown. Sprinkle vegetables with flour, stir, and continue to cook over low heat for 10 minutes. Do not brown. Add chilled chicken stock and bring to a boil, stirring constantly. Reduce to a simmer and add potatoes. Tie thyme, bay leaf, marjoram, parsley, peppercorns, and garlic in a cheesecloth and add to simmering soup. Remove corn from cob with a sharp knife; add corn to soup. Simmer until potatoes are tender. Add half-and-half or light cream and return to simmer. Season with salt and white pepper to taste. Ladle into soup bowls and garnish with a dollop of butter.

Yield: 8 to 10 servings

Cashew Soup

This simple recipe from the White Cloud Natural Foods Inn, in Newfoundland, Pennsylvania, recalls in spirit the bounteous natural feasts of early Thanksgivings. It is an ideal first course for a vegetarian holiday feast.

1 heaping tsp poultry seasoning
1 scant tsp curry powder
1 tsp salt
1 cup roasted unsalted cashews

4 cups water or soup stock
chopped chives (for garnish)
paprika (for garnish)

Put all ingredients in stockpot and bring to a boil. Pour the mixture into blender and puree until smooth. Pour into bowls and garnish with chives and paprika. Serve immediately.

Yield: 4 servings

NOTE: This recipe can be doubled. If the entire amount will not fit into blender, prepare in two batches and mix both batches of the soup together before serving.

King's Arms Tavern
Cream of Peanut Soup

Peanuts did not become a staple in the American diet until after the Civil War. By the turn of the century, however, they appeared in many courses of the most elegant meals. At Colonial Williamsburg, which prepares traditional, bounteous late-nineteenth century feasts, this soup is a favorite. Try it with freshly ground peanut butter (available at health food stores) and don't forget the sippets (p. 25) to soak up the leftovers.

1 medium onion, chopped
2 ribs of celery, chopped
¼ cup butter
3 tbsp all-purpose flour
2 qt chicken stock or
  canned chicken broth

2 cups smooth peanut butter
1 ¾ cups light cream
chopped peanuts (for garnish)

Sauté onion and celery in butter until soft, but not brown. Stir in the flour until well blended. Add chicken stock, stirring constantly, and bring to a boil. Remove from the heat and puree in food processor or blender. Add peanut butter and light cream, stirring to blend thoroughly. Return to low heat and heat until just hot (about 10 minutes). Do not boil.

Garnish with peanuts and serve immediately.

Yield: 10 to 12 servings

NOTE: This soup is also good served ice-cold.

Sippets

Since the seventeenth century, the term ''sippets'' has described strips of toast used to sop up soup or broth. At holiday celebrations in Colonial Williamsburg, sippets are served with the village's classic King's Arms Tavern Cream of Peanut Soup (p. 24). Try them this year to add an elegant colonial touch to your holiday first course.

6 ½-inch thick slices of firm white bread

Trim crusts and cut each slice into 4 horizontal strips. Brown the sippets in the oven or toast lightly for 2 to 3 minutes.

Yield: 24 sippets

Mushrooms à la Millbrook

This recent creation of Vermont's Millbrook Lodge blends two of the lodge's specialties: mouthwatering appetizers and its trademark Millbrook Anadama Bread (p. 72). The ground veal and wine bring subtle but hearty flavors to this impressive beginning to a Thanksgiving banquet.

30 large mushrooms
¼ lb veal, ground
1 clove garlic
¼ medium onion, chopped
2 tsp olive oil
¼ cup red wine
¼ tsp oregano
¼ tsp parsley

¼ tsp rosemary
¼ tsp basil
¼ tsp sage
¼ cup Anadama Bread crumbs
  (p. 72) or any flavored bread crumbs
salt and pepper to taste
1 egg, lightly beaten

Wash and dry the mushrooms. Carefully remove stems and set aside. Mix together ground veal, garlic, and onion. Heat the olive oil in a 10½-inch frying pan. When oil begins to smoke, immediately add ground veal mixture. Cook at high heat until the meat loses its pinkness. Still at high heat, add the wine and deglaze the pan. Reduce the liquid to half, then lower heat and add all the herbs, bread crumbs, salt, and pepper. Turn off heat and add the egg. Mix well. Stuff each mushroom cap and serve on decorative platter.

Yield: 6 servings

Dungeness Crab Legs with Crab Cream

As the Thanksgiving holiday season approaches on the West Coast, the Dungeness crab season is just beginning. The Carter House Bed and Breakfast Inn, in Eureka, California, takes advantage of this bounty in this luscious recipe.

2 sticks plus 2 tbsp unsalted butter
1 small white onion, sliced thin
1 tsp rosemary
3 tbsp parsley, chopped
½ cup white wine
¼ lb crab meat
½ cup cream

10 oz fresh spinach
½ tsp nutmeg
30 to 36 Dungeness crab legs
juice of one lemon
salt to taste
freshly ground pepper to taste

In a large pan, melt one stick of butter and sauté onion until translucent. Add rosemary and parsley. Stir in the white wine and reduce the heat to a simmer. Add crabmeat to mixture and simmer for five minutes, stirring occasionally. Strain the mixture thoroughly and return to pan. Reduce liquid by two-thirds and remove from heat. Stir in cream and set aside.

Bring four quarts of water to boil. Place spinach in water and boil until tender. Drain spinach. Puree spinach, ½ stick of butter, and nutmeg in blender or food processor. Set pureed spinach aside.

In a medium-sized skillet, melt 6 tablespoons of butter. Add the crab legs, lemon juice, and salt and pepper. Sauté for 5 to 10 minutes.

To serve, pour 2 to 3 tablespoons of crab cream in the center of each plate and arrange 5 or 6 legs into a starburst around it. Spoon the pureed spinach into the center of each of the starbursts. Grind pepper over the entire plate for garnish and serve.

Yield: 6 servings

The Great Turkey Controversy

"A Meeting of Minds," late nineteenth century, artist unknown
(Culver Pictures)

Turkeys are as American as apple pie. No other country makes such a fuss about its native bird. Explorers to America praised the turkey, Indians feared it, and Benjamin Franklin, the turkey's greatest champion, immortalized it as a "bird of courage" and a "true, original native of America who would not hesitate to attack a grenadier of the British guard who should presume to invade the farmyard with a red coat on."

But while everyone agrees that the turkey is the perfect food for Thanksgiving, no one seems to be able to agree on *the* way to cook it. There are the basters, the non-basters, the wrap-it-in-aluminum-foilers, and the oiled-paper-baggers. Some swear by paprika, others abhor it. Others love Aunty Em's favorite recipe, and still others, tuned to the latest in culinary arts, think nothing of cooking the family bird, complete with wild rice and green grapes, in a microwave.

In the following pages there are three distinctly different turkey recipes, and instructions on a variety of cooking methods. Each version can be served with any of the mouthwatering side dishes and stuffings you will find in later sections.

Choose the turkey recipe that beckons. Just make sure that there's enough for seconds!

"For turkey braised, the Lord be praised."

—from a nineteenth-century guide to turkey preparations

Turkey Tips

- Though it may take some searching, try to buy fresh turkey this Thanksgiving. It makes for a taste treat!

- When purchasing a turkey, allow 1 to 1 ½ pounds per person. Allow ¾ pound of stuffing per person.

- Thaw the turkey in an unopened wrapper on a tray in the refrigerator, according to package directions or instructions from your butcher. DO NOT THAW AT ROOM TEMPERATURE.

- Should plans change after the turkey is partially thawed, it may be refrozen if it has not been held for more than one to two days in the refrigerator. Place it directly on the floor of the freezer so the bird will refreeze as rapidly as possible. While this is said to be a safe practice, the quality of the turkey will decline.

- Do not stuff the bird before you are ready to roast it. Refrigerating a stuffed, raw bird is unadvisable; the stuffing is a prime breeding ground for bacteria.

- Do not partially cook turkey one day and complete the cooking the next day. Day-ahead cooking will not shorten the cooking time, because it takes just as long the second day to bring the internal temperature up to the recommended range as it does to cook the turkey initially. Furthermore, bacteria may multiply in the stuffing during two-day roasting.

- After roasting, let the bird rest at least 15 minutes before carving. If your guests are late, do not panic; a cooked bird will stay quite warm for up to one hour if covered with aluminum foil. Once you have displayed your turkey for everyone to see, carve it away from the table. While the whole roast turkey was lovely and the expertly carved meat will be elegant, carving can be an unattractive job. Once you are ready to carve, follow these seven easy steps for a perfectly carved bird:

  1. Have a clean serving platter ready.
  2. Use your sharpest carving knife; it will make your job easier and will make the turkey go further.
  3. Sever the drumsticks at the joints.
  4. Remove the wings.

5. Carve the turkey. Steady the bird by inserting a two-pronged carving fork in the breast, as near to the ridge (breastbone) as possible. Make a long, horizontal cut near the rib cage, so that as you proceed to carve, the meat will fall from the bird freely. Begin at the area nearest the neck and slice thinly across the grain, the entire length of the breast. Repeat on the other side, if desired.
6. Detach the thighs from the carcass and slice or leave whole, as desired.
7. Arrange carved meat on a platter and garnish with parsley sprigs, orange slices, and raw cranberries, if desired.

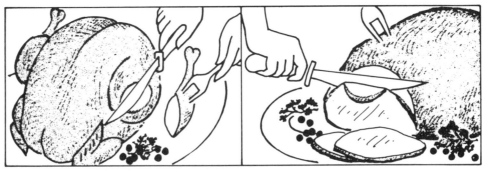

Drawings by Jane Eldershaw

- After serving the turkey, treat it right. Remove any remaining stuffing and refrigerate in a covered bowl or wrap it securely and freeze it. Use refrigerated stuffing within three days, frozen stuffing within one month. The whole turkey or meat cut from the bones may be refrigerated or wrapped and frozen. Refrigerated meat will remain fresh for three days, frozen meat for two months.

- Unless everyone has picked them clean, you can make an easy but satisfying soup or stock from the turkey bones. To prepare Thanksgiving Night Soup, sauté 2 chopped onions, 2 diced carrots, 2 ribs of celery, and 2 minced cloves of garlic in 2 tablespoons of butter until the onions begin to brown. Add turkey bones and cover with water. Cover the saucepan and bring ingredients to a boil. Reduce to a simmer and cook for 1½ to 2 hours. Season with salt, pepper, parsley, and thyme as desired. For a heartier soup, add leftover gravy and stuffing or use the soup as a full-bodied broth for Turkey Barley Chowder (p. 72) and Garden-Patch Turkey Stew with Dumplings (p. 71).

- For packing lunches, turkey sandwiches (minus mayonnaise and lettuce) freeze well. They will thaw by noon and will be ready for eating; at the same time, they will help keep other foods cool.

Basting the Turkey

To children on Thanksgiving, watching the turkey being basted is one of the most fascinating parts of the day. The baster looks like a toy and the whole process looks like great fun! To the cook, however, basting can be a mystery. How often do you baste? How much? With what?

Basting a turkey *does* make a difference. It prevents the bird from drying out and adds to its overall flavor. Most turkeys should be basted once every 15 to 20 minutes, with a turkey baster or a long-handled brush. Simply spread the juices in the pan over the body of the bird, making sure to reach all over.

While the turkey's own juices are sufficient for basting, you can subtly accent the bird's flavor by trying the following variations:

- turkey broth (from giblets boiled in water)
- a sweet country mixture of one part honey or maple syrup to one part water, applied after the turkey has roasted for one hour
- chicken broth laced with cayenne or jalapeño pepper
- an Oriental broth of one part soy, one part sesame oil, and two parts water.

THE AMERICAN EAGLE AND THE THANKSGIVING TURKEY

"May one give us peace in all our states,
The other a piece for all our plates—"

—from a nineteenth-century postcard

Contrary to folklore, Benjamin Franklin never lobbied for the turkey to appear on the Great Seal. It was never mentioned in the meetings on the design of the Great Seal, which, when adopted in 1782, honored the bald eagle. Franklin wanted the illustration for the seal to show the parting of the Red Sea and destruction of the Pharaoh's chariots, with the inscription "Rebellion to tyrants is obedience to God."

Turkey Roasting Methods

NOTES

• Standard roasting time for bird under 16 pounds—15 min/lb
  Standard roasting time for bird over 16 pounds—12 min/lb

• For a moist turkey, baste every 15 to 20 minutes with pan drippings
  or other basting sauces.

• If using meat thermometer, insert it in the center of the thigh muscle, not touching the bone.

CONVENTIONAL OVEN—OPEN PAN

Roast turkey, breast up, on flat rack in shallow open pan in preheated 325° oven. Baste every 15-20 minutes.

This dry-heat method is the easiest method for turkey roasting. The turkey requires only minimal handling and turns out to be golden brown, attractive, with a rich roasted flavor.

CONVENTIONAL OVEN—HIGH HEAT FIRST

Place well-basted turkey in shallow pan, breast up. Roast in preheated 450° oven for 30 minutes. Reduce heat to 325° and continue roasting.

This has become a favorite method for producing an evenly browned bird that is juicy and moist.

CONVENTIONAL OVEN—COVERED PAN

Cook turkey, breast up, in covered dark enamel pan in 325° oven.

With this method, the cooking time is shortened, but the bird becomes less attractive in appearance than with the Open Pan method. This moist heat method often produces uneven browning and does not give the turkey a roasted flavor.

CONVENTIONAL OVEN—OVEN COOKING BAG

Place the turkey, breast up, in a floured plastic cooking bag in shallow open pan. Close bag loosely and make slits in top of bag with knife. Cook in 350° oven.

The turkey cooks in drippings trapped in bag. While this method is simple, with little cleanup required, the turkey is less attractive and lacks roasted flavor.

CONVENTIONAL OVEN—FOIL-WRAPPED

Place the *unstuffed* turkey, breast up, on foil. Wrap loosely and cook in shallow pan in 450° oven.

This moist-heat method reduces the cooking time, but the turkey may cook unevenly. Be sure to check final internal temperature of thigh and breast. This method is to be used only on an unstuffed turkey.

CONVENTIONAL OVEN—CLAY POT

Place the turkey, breast up, in presoaked covered clay pot in cold oven. Cook at 450°.

The turkey browns evenly with this shortened cooking time method. A meat thermometer is essential to ensure that thigh, breast, and stuffing reach recommended final temperatures.

MICROWAVE OVEN

Cook the stuffed or unstuffed turkey, breast down, at high, 4 minutes per pound, and then, breast up, at medium (50% power), 8 minutes per pound.

This cool-cooking method roasts a turkey 12 pounds and under in about half the time, but it requires extra handling during cooking. Be sure to use a browning sauce for even color.

COVERED KETTLE CHARCOAL GRILL

Place *unstuffed* turkey, breast up, on rack over drip pan with 25 hot coals on each of two sides. Add briquettes and turn every hour.

Barbecued turkey from the grill is very attractive, and it has a delicious smoked flavor. Do not prepare a stuffed turkey on the grill, however; the stuffing takes on a strong smoked taste that obscures its more subtle flavors.

CHARCOAL WATER SMOKE COOKER

Place unstuffed turkey on rack over water pan and hot coals with wet wood to generate smoke. Cover. Add briquettes as required.

Turkey will become dark brown, with a distinct smoky flavor. For food safety, turkey must pass through the critical range of 45° to 140° in less than 4 hours.

Classic Roast Turkey

The perfect roast turkey recipe yields a bird that is tender, succulent, and brimming with juices for gravy. This recipe does that, and more. You will find it easy to follow and simple to adapt to your favorite holiday herbs and spices.

ROAST STUFFED TURKEY

1 turkey	*salt to taste*
stuffing of your choice (pp. 41-44)	*freshly ground pepper to taste*
⅛-¼ lb butter, depending	*¼ cup water*
on size of turkey	

Preheat oven to 325°.

Rinse the turkey and pat it dry. Stuff the body and neck cavities before trussing. Soften butter and rub all over the turkey—it should be thoroughly buttered. Sprinkle with salt and pepper and place, breast down, on greased rack in pan with ¼ cup water. Baste turkey every 20 minutes with this mixture until enough pan drippings for basting have accumulated in bottom of roasting pan. Cook 15 minutes per pound if turkey weighs less than 16 pounds, 12 minutes per pound if it is heavier. Turn breast up after 1 hour if turkey weighs less than 12 pounds; after 1½ hours if the turkey weighs more. When a meat thermometer registers 170° in the breast meat and 180° in the thigh meat, remove the turkey to a warm platter and cover loosely with a towel or foil. Prepare gravy, if desired (p. 35). Let rest 15 minutes before carving (p. 30).

UNSTUFFED ROAST TURKEY

Omit the stuffing. Sprinkle the body cavity with 1 teaspoon salt and ½ teaspoon poultry seasoning, then place in the cavity 5 sprigs parsley, 4 stalks celery, and 3 onions, apples, or oranges, quartered. Follow roasting directions for Roast Stuffed Turkey.

Yield: Allow 1-1½ lbs per person

Classic Pan Gravy with Giblets

1 tbsp butter
1 onion, minced
1 carrot, diced
giblets, removed from turkey cavity,
  rinsed; neck cut in half

4 cups water
3 tbsp flour
salt and pepper to taste

WHILE THE TURKEY ROASTS:

Melt butter in saucepan over medium heat; add onion and carrot, and sauté 10 minutes. Add giblets and water. Cover and cook over low heat for 1 hour, or until meat is easily removed from neck. Strain and reserve broth. Remove meat from neck; mince it and other giblets. Return giblets to broth and set aside.

WHEN THE TURKEY HAS ROASTED:

Remove the turkey from the roasting pan, leaving juices in the pan. Place roasting pan directly on low to medium heat; holding it firmly, use wooden spoon to scrape and mix all pan juices as they begin to boil. Sprinkle flour into juices and continue to stir until flour and juices are combined and no particles stick to the bottom. Slowly add broth and stir until mixed. Let boil 2 minutes. Salt and pepper to taste. Warm as needed.

Yield: 4 cups gravy

"You first parents of the human race . . . who ruined
yourself for an apple, what might you not have done
for a truffled turkey?"

—Anthelme Brillat-Savarin, French food writer

Roast Turkey with
Lemon and Ham Stuffing Balls

This 150-year-old recipe is a favorite from Massachusetts' Old Sturbridge Village and reveals a long-lost method of preparing stuffing. Instead of serving stuffing in a casserole, it is shaped into small balls, browned in butter, and later used as an elegant garnish for the turkey platter.

1 10-lb turkey
¾ tsp salt
¼ tsp freshly ground pepper

¼ cup unsifted all-purpose flour
½ pound unsalted butter, melted
 (for basting)

LEMON AND HAM STUFFING BALLS

6 cups soft fine bread crumbs
1 cup firmly packed ground suet,
 lard, or vegetable shortening
1 ¼ cups minced ham,
 both Smithfield and Virginia
2 ½ tsp marjoram
rind of 1 large lemon, finely grated
juice of 1 large lemon

1 ½ tsp salt
⅛ tsp freshly ground pepper
⅛ tsp freshly grated nutmeg
2 egg yolks
¼ cup unsalted butter, melted
 (for browning stuffing balls)

GIBLET GRAVY

turkey neck and giblets
6 cups water
7 tbsp turkey pan drippings

6 tbsp flour
½ tsp salt
⅛ tsp pepper

Preheat oven to 325°.

Rub the turkey inside and out with salt and pepper, then rub turkey skin all over with flour to coat evenly and lightly. Prepare the stuffing by mixing together with your hands the bread crumbs, suet, ham, marjoram, lemon rind, lemon juice, salt, pepper, nutmeg, and egg yolks. Fork up mixture so that it is fluffy, and drop lightly into both neck and body cavities of the turkey. Refrigerate remaining stuffing until about an hour before serving. Skewer neck skin of turkey flat to the back, enclosing stuffing in neck cavity, then lace the body cavity shut with poultry pins and twine. Truss the turkey so that it is as compact as possible. Place breast side up on a rack in a large, shallow roasting pan and roast, uncovered, for 1 hour. Baste lavishly with melted butter and roast about 2 hours longer, basting often with remaining butter and pan drippings, until turkey is richly browned and the leg joint moves easily.

While turkey roasts, prepare the stock for gravy. Place turkey neck and giblets in large, heavy stockpan, add the water, and simmer, uncovered, for 20 minutes; remove liver and heart and refrigerate. Continue to simmer neck and gizzard as long as turkey roasts; discard neck and mince gizzard, liver, and heart. Strain turkey stock, measure out 2½ cups, and add the minced gizzard, liver, and heart (save any remaining stock to use in soups or sauces later).

About 1 hour before the turkey has finished roasting, shape the remaining stuffing into balls about the size of crab apples (1½ to 2 inches in diameter) and brown lightly in a skillet in the ¼ cup melted butter. Transfer balls to a small baking pan, arranging one layer deep. Pour any skillet drippings over balls, cover snugly with foil, and set in oven with turkey to bake for 1 hour. When turkey is done (it will take about 3 hours for a 10-pound bird), remove from oven and let rest 20 minutes on the kitchen counter so that juices will settle and carving will be easier. Turn oven off but leave stuffing balls in oven to keep warm.

To make the gravy, quickly skim 7 tablespoons of fat from the drippings into a medium-sized saucepan and blend in the flour. Heat and stir until mixture begins to turn a pale brown. Add the 2½ cups giblet stock and minced giblets. Heat and stir until mixture thickens, about 2 to 3 minutes. Turn heat to lowest point, add salt and pepper, and let gravy mellow until you are ready to serve the turkey.

Remove twine and poultry pins from turkey; arrange on a heated large platter. Surround with stuffing balls, sprigs of watercress, and, for added color, clusters of whole raw cranberries. Pour gravy into gravy boat and pass.

Yield: 6 to 8 servings

Boned Turkey
with Vegetable Stuffing

This recipe is the 1986 first-prize winner of Gravymaster's "Best of the Bird" contest. This yearly contest rates turkeys prepared by many of the top student chefs at New York metropolitan area culinary schools. To ease your preparation of this grand dish, you may want to ask your butcher to provide you with an already boned turkey.

12-lb turkey, deboned
1 tbsp browning sauce
(such as Gravy Master)

1 tbsp honey

VEGETABLE STUFFING

¾ cup water
juice of 1 lemon
10 large mushrooms
3 small leeks,
* trimmed to 8 inches in length*
2 small summer squash, cut into strips
2 small carrots, peeled and quartered
2 tbsp butter

1 onion, coarsely chopped
3 cloves garlic, finely chopped
1½ pounds spinach,
* stemmed and cleaned*
¾ cup grated Parmesan cheese
½ tsp nutmeg
salt and pepper to taste
2 egg whites

TURKEY VEGETABLE SAUCE

2 carrots, cut into ½-inch pieces
1 celery stalk, cut into 1-inch pieces
2 large onions, cut into 1-inch pieces
3 cloves garlic, halved
1 tbsp safflower oil
turkey bones, neck, wings, heart,
* and gizzard*

1 bay leaf
2 tsp fresh thyme
¾ cup red wine
1½ cups chopped mushrooms
1 tsp browning sauce
* (such as Gravy Master)*
salt and pepper to taste

Preheat oven to 400°.

Prepare stock for sauce. Place carrots, celery, onions, and garlic in roasting pan and toss with oil. Cut turkey bones and neck into pieces and place over vegetables along with wings, heart, and gizzard. Roast until bones are brown, about 30 minutes. Reduce oven to 350° for turkey. Transfer bones and vegetables to large pot. Deglaze roasting pan with 2 cups of water and add liquid to pot. Add bay leaf and thyme. Bring stock to a boil, reduce to simmer for 1½ hours. Then strain stock into saucepan. Add wine, mushrooms, salt, and pepper. Simmer until reduced to about 2 cups. Add browning sauce to pan and simmer for 10 minutes. Puree sauce in a food processor and serve in gravy boat.

To prepare vegetable stuffing, heat ¾ cup water with lemon juice over medium heat. Add mushrooms, leeks, and dash of salt. Cover and cook for 7 minutes. Stir and lay summer squash strips on top and continue cooking for 5 minutes. Drain and discard liquid. Cook carrots in fresh water until tender. Melt butter in skillet over medium heat and cook onion and garlic, stirring occasionally, until translucent. Cook spinach in boiling water for 2 minutes, drain and cool with cold water. Form balls of spinach with your hands. Slice balls into thin sections. Put slices in a large mixing bowl and combine with Parmesan cheese. Add nutmeg, pepper, salt, and sautéed onion and garlic. Whip egg whites until foamy and add to spinach mixture.

To stuff turkey, lay bird out on flat surface. Sprinkle meat with salt and pepper. Spread spinach mixture evenly to 1 inch from edges. Lay on alternating strips of squash, carrot, and leek. Arrange mushrooms in row in center. Wrap meat up around stuffing and sew together with skewers, closing all holes. Place bird on a rack in roasting pan. Make cooking tent out of foil and lay shiny side down over turkey, tucking the sides loosely inside the pan. Cook for 45 minutes. Remove pan from oven and reduce temperature to 325°. Take off tent and brush the outside of the turkey with a mixture of browning sauce and honey. Return turkey to oven for 45 minutes to 1 hour. Cut finished turkey into ¼-inch slices and serve.

Yield: 10 servings

> *"The black turkey gobbler, the tips of his beautiful tail;*
> *above us the dark became yellow.*
> *The sunbeams stream forward."*
> —Black Turkey Gobbler Chant (Apache)

He enters upon this world of trouble.

He sees astonishing sights.

He makes his first acquaintance with his enemy, man.

Time passes, and he is enabled to have revenge.

He gobbles well.

But he is gobbled.

"The Career of a Turkey," *Harper's Weekly,* November 30, 1867 (Picture collection, the Branch Libraries, the New York Public Library)

Thanksgiving Stuffings

Czechoslovakian Dressing

Over the years, Thanksgiving celebrations across the country have taken on distinctly ethnic flavors; immigrants adapted back-home recipes to American tastes and cooking styles. At Schumacher's New Prague Hotel, in New Prague, Minnesota, Bohemia mixes with New England in a Thanksgiving feast that shares as much with Oktoberfest as it would have with the Pilgrims. The hotel's menu features German and Czech touches, beginning with the roast goose and dressing. The executive chef, John Schumacher, says that the sauerkraut-and-potato-based Czechoslovakian Dressing complements all fowl.

½ cup sugar
1 tbsp flour
⅓ tsp caraway seeds
1 tsp chicken base
½ tsp salt

½ tsp white pepper
4 cups sauerkraut, washed and drained
1 cup grated raw potatoes
1 cup diced unpeeled apples
½ cup diced peaches (drained)

Mix sugar, flour, caraway seeds, chicken base, salt, and pepper together. Set aside. Drain and wash sauerkraut and grated potatoes. In large bowl, add sauerkraut, grated potatoes, apples, and peaches. Mix well by hand. Add spices and mix well.

Yield: 6 cups, enough for an 8-lb turkey

Grandma Hepford's Oyster and Chestnut Stuffings

Grandma Neta Hoffman Hepford lived in a large house outside of Philadelphia around the turn of the century. She always made a point of using only the finest fresh ingredients in her cooking. Her traditional Philadelphia stuffings are no exception. Philadelphia dressings for turkey are very different from dressings made in other parts of the country. In New England, a bread dressing is popular; in Boston, because of the Irish influence, a potato dressing is used. In the South, it's often cornbread. Philadelphians are partial to oyster and chestnut dressings.

GRANDMA HEPFORD'S OYSTER STUFFING

3 cups soft bread crumbs	*a few drops of onion juice*
1 tbsp chopped parsley	*21 oysters, shucked*
1 tsp salt	*¼ cup oyster liquor*
¼ tsp pepper	*2 tbsp unsalted butter*

In a mixing bowl, combine the bread crumbs, parsley, salt, pepper, and onion juice. Clean the oysters of any bits of shell, then add them to the crumb mixture. Heat the oyster liquor, add the butter, and stir until melted. Pour over crumb mixture and mix thoroughly. Cool completely, then use it to stuff poultry.

Yield: 4½ cups, enough for a 6-lb turkey

> *"Lord, behold our family here assembled. We thank Thee*
> *for this place in which we dwell; for the love that unites us;*
> *for the peace accorded us this day; for the hope with which*
> *we expect tomorrow; for the health, the work, the food, and*
> *the bright skies, that make our lives delightful; for our friends*
> *in all parts of the earth, and our friendly helpers . . .*
> *Let Peace abound in our small company."*
> —Robert Louis Stevenson

GRANDMA HEPFORD'S CHESTNUT STUFFING

2 cups chestnuts   *1 tsp salt*
3 tbsp unsalted butter   *¼ tsp pepper*
Salt and pepper to taste   *butter to taste*
1 cup soft bread crumbs   *¼ cup hot milk*

Place chestnuts in saucepan, add 4 cups boiling water, and simmer for 3 minutes. Drain and spread blanched nuts on paper towels. Let them dry overnight.

The next day, place chestnuts in saucepan and cover with 4 cups of lightly salted boiling water. Cover and simmer for 10 to 15 minutes. Drain, peel, and mash the chestnuts to a paste, or finely grind by hand or in food processor. Season to taste with butter, salt, and pepper.

In mixing bowl, combine bread crumbs, salt, and pepper. In small saucepan, melt butter in milk, and pour over bread crumbs. Add chestnut mixture and mix thoroughly. Cool completely, then use it to stuff poultry.

Yield: 3 cups, enough for a 4-lb turkey

Whole Wheat Stuffing

Chewy, flavorful whole wheat bread adds a healthy zip to the Thanksgiving dish that many holiday feasters love most. For variety, prepare with fresh pecans or cashews.

8 cups day-old whole wheat   *3 tbsp unsalted butter*
  bread, cubed   *1 ¼ cups chicken broth*
1 tsp salt   *1 cup white wine*
1 tsp pepper   *½ cup walnut pieces, toasted*
1 cup chopped celery   *and coarsely chopped*
¾ cup finely sliced green   *2 eggs, beaten lightly*
  onions (scallions)   *2 tsp sage*

Preheat oven to 400°.

In large mixing bowl, combine bread, salt, and pepper. Sauté celery and onions on medium high heat, about 10 minutes, or until onions wilt. Add mixture to the bread. Mix in other ingredients and place stuffing in 3-quart baking dish. Bake for 25 to 30 minutes, until the top is well browned.

Yield: 9 cups, enough for a 12-lb turkey

Canadian Wild Rice Dressing with Cranberries

At the Amherst Shore Country Inn, in Amherst, Nova Scotia, Canadian Wild Rice Dressing with Cranberries is truly a hometown creation. The innkeepers buy locally grown wild rice and pick wild cranberries from nearby patches. Traditionally, this savory dressing is served with Cornish hen. It is also ideal for turkey and game, or for serving as a side dish.

1 ½ cups wild rice, rinsed
generous dash of salt
6 tbsp long-grain white rice
1 cup chicken stock
1 cup fresh cranberries, sliced

2 tbsp white sugar
1 tbsp Grand Marnier liqueur
2 tbsp orange juice
1 tbsp orange peel, coarsely grated

In a large saucepan, cook wild rice in 3 cups boiling water and salt for about one hour. The rice will split and curl. Add additional water if necessary. Drain, rinse, and set aside.

Simmer long-grain rice in chicken stock for 20 to 25 minutes. Combine with wild rice and cool. Stir in sliced cranberries, sugar, Grand Marnier, orange juice, and orange peel.

Yield: 6 cups, enough for an 8-lb turkey or for 4 Cornish hens

NOTE: If dressing is to be used as a side dish, place it in ovenproof casserole and bake in moderate oven (350°) for 30 minutes.

If dressing is to be used for Cornish hens, wash four hens inside and out. Pat dry. Sprinkle cavity with salt. Divide dressing among the birds and stuff lightly. Close with skewer. Place birds in foil-lined baking dish. Baste generously with a combination of melted butter and orange juice (½ cup of each). Cover loosely with foil and bake at 350° for ½ hour. Remove foil and bake an additional 1 to 1 ¼ hours, basting frequently until tender and golden brown.

"Thanksgiving day, I fear,
If one solemn truth must touch,
Is celebrated, not so much
To thank the Lord for blessings o'er,
As for the sake of getting more!"
—Will Carleton, American poet

A Holiday Change of Pace

Shaker Sausage and Oyster Loaf

Thanksgiving was an important Shaker holiday. At the end of the harvest, the farmers had much to be thankful for, and they celebrated their bounty with a Thanksgiving dinner that featured recipes with unusual ingredients. Their dinner loaf, brimming with sausages and oysters, and accented with spices and horseradish, is but one of several main courses that would grace the Thanksgiving table. For a Shaker-style Thanksgiving, serve the loaf with Scalloped Corn (p. 49) and Date-Pecan Pudding (p. 61).

1 pint raw oysters, shucked
1 lb bulk sausage
2 cups soft bread crumbs
2 eggs, beaten

1 heaping tsp Shaker herb salt,
  or equal portions basil, thyme,
  rosemary, and dill, mixed
2 tsp catsup
2 tbsp horseradish

Preheat oven to 350°.

Grind or chop oysters and mix thoroughly by hand with sausage meat. Add bread crumbs and beaten eggs. Stir in herb mix, catsup, and horseradish. Mix well and pack into a 4½ ″x 8″ bread pan. Bake 30 minutes, or until loaf leaves edges of pan. As meat cooks, drain off half the accumulated fat, or enough to keep loaf moist.

Serve with warm hollandaise sauce.

Yield: 6 to 8 servings

HOLLANDAISE SAUCE

3 egg yolks
1 tbsp lemon juice
¼ lb butter, melted

2 tbsp hot water
dash of cayenne pepper
salt to taste

In a double boiler or metal bowl placed over hot, but not simmering, water, place egg yolks in boiler top and beat with a wire whisk until smooth. Add lemon juice and gradually whisk in melted butter. Slowly stir in hot water, cayenne pepper, and salt. Continue to mix for 1 minute, until thickened. Serve immediately.

Yield: 1 cup

Hazelnut Chicken with Orange Thyme Cream

Jeffrey P. Houston, the chef at Shelter Harbor Inn, in Westerly, Rhode Island, says that this recipe is perfect for an intimate Thanksgiving dinner. He suggests wild rice as an accompaniment.

2 whole bòned chicken breasts,
  skinned and lightly pounded

flour to dredge
3 tbsp butter

HAZELNUT CRUMB MIXTURE

⅓ cup hazelnuts, coarsely chopped
⅓ cup fresh bread crumbs
¼ tsp thyme

1 egg, lightly beaten with
  1 tsp water
salt and pepper to taste

ORANGE THYME CREAM

1 orange, sectioned
  (reserve any juice)
⅛ tsp thyme
1 tbsp hazelnut liqueur
  (such as Frangelico)

1 cup heavy cream
salt and pepper to taste

Cut each chicken breast in half. Mix together hazelnut pieces, bread crumbs, and thyme. Set aside. Prepare egg wash. Beat egg lightly with water, and add salt and pepper.

Dredge chicken breasts in flour, dip into egg wash, and coat with hazelnut crumb mixture. Shake off excess. Chill until ready to use.

Melt butter in heavy pan. Over moderate heat, cook chicken breasts until golden brown on both sides, approximately 10 to 15 minutes. Add reserved orange juice, thyme, hazelnut liqueur, and heavy cream. Simmer gently, basting often, until chicken is barely cooked through and sauce has thickened slightly. Add orange sections and season to taste with salt and pepper.

Remove chicken breasts from pan and pour sauce over them. Serve immediately.

Yield: 2 servings

Baked Nut Loaf

This hearty vegetarian standard takes the place of roast turkey at White Cloud Inn, in the Pocono Mountains of Pennsylvania. Cashew Soup (p. 24), homemade cranberry relish, and whole wheat bread round out this homestyle natural foods menu.

½ cup chopped onion
½ cup diced celery
1 tbsp oil
1 cup chopped nuts (walnuts and
  cashews), finely chopped
1 cup cottage cheese
½ tsp salt

1 cup bread crumbs
2 eggs, lightly beaten
¼ tsp poultry seasoning
1 ¼ tsp onion powder
⅔ cup water

Preheat oven to 375°.

Sauté onion and celery in oil. Put all ingredients into a greased 11¾″ × 7½″ baking dish and bake until just firm and slightly brown on top, about 35 to 40 minutes.

Serve with your favorite sauce or gravy. The Inn uses a mushroom sauce, but the dish is also good with a tomato sauce or onion gravy.

Yield: 5 to 6 servings

Mennonite Skillet Chicken with Sour Cream

"Let the guest sojourning here know that in this home our life is simple. What we cannot afford we do not offer, but what good cheer we can give, we give gladly."
—Sign welcoming visitors to Patchwork Quilt Country Inn,
Middlebury, Indiana

Hearty food in abundance is the specialty at the century-old Patchwork Quilt Country Inn. This prizewinning regional creation was inspired by Amish and Mennonite communities in the area. Innkeeper Michele Lovejoy Goebel serves this dish in individual-sized cast-iron skillets.

½ cup butter	paprika
¼ cup all-purpose flour	½ cup water
2 tsp salt	2 tbsp flour
dash of pepper	1 cup sour cream
2 2½-lb broilers,	parsley
cut in quarters	spiced crab apples (optional)

Preheat oven to 325°.

Melt butter in cast-iron skillet. Combine ¼ cup flour, salt, and pepper in separate dish. Coat chicken in the flour mixture, making certain that each piece is completely covered. Dip the coated pieces in the melted butter, coating all sides, and arrange skin side up in the skillet. Sprinkle with paprika. Bake in oven for 1½ hours, or until chicken is tender and golden brown. Remove chicken from skillet and keep warm.

Add water to drippings in the skillet and mix well. Blend in 2 tablespoons flour, ½ teaspoon salt, a dash each of pepper and paprika, and sour cream. Bring to a boil, stirring constantly. Remove from heat as soon as it begins to boil. Return chicken to skillet. Cover with gravy and sprinkle with additional paprika. Garnish with parsley and spiced crab apples. Serve in the cast-iron skillet.

Yield: 8 servings

Side Dishes and Vegetables

Shaker Scalloped Corn

Corn was a staple in the Shaker community. The Shakers raised and canned it, and also sold it to the public. At their own table, they served it in a simple manner. But on holidays, they prepared special creations, such as this one. The Shakers served scalloped corn with almost any festive main course; it makes a particularly good complement to roast turkey and pork.

12 strips bacon, fried crisp
4 tbsp bacon fat
1 large green pepper, chopped
1 large onion, sliced
3 cups fresh corn, mixed
* with 1 cup milk or cream,*
* or 2 15½-oz cans*
* cream-style corn*

1½ cups fine bread crumbs
2 eggs, beaten
1½ cups light cream
1 tsp salt
½ tsp pepper
butter

Preheat oven to 375°, and grease casserole dish with butter.

Fry bacon and remove from grease. When cool, break into small pieces. Using 4 tablespoons of bacon grease, sauté green pepper and onion. Add corn, bread crumbs, beaten egg, light cream, salt, pepper, and bacon pieces.

Dot with plenty of butter and bake for approximately 20 minutes, until very hot and bubbly all the way through. Crumbs should be nicely browned.

Yield: 8 to 10 servings

Cool Cucumbers with Hot Pepper

On the night before the big day, take a break from holiday baking and prepare this cooling salad. It will be a light and zesty counterpoint to your more substantial holiday offerings.

4 cucumbers, peeled
¼ tsp salt
½ cup water
½ cup white vinegar
½ cup sugar
¼ tsp cayenne pepper
(or more, to taste)

¼ cup chopped fresh coriander
  or 1 tsp ground
salt to taste
chopped red pepper or
  cherry tomato halves (for garnish)

Slice cucumbers; set aside in colander. Add salt and let drain for 30 to 60 minutes. In a saucepan, combine water, vinegar, sugar, and cayenne and bring to a boil. Let cool completely to room temperature. Toss cucumbers to release additional water; transfer to bowl. Add coriander, then vinegar solution. Refrigerate at least 2 hours. Taste for seasoning before serving. Garnish with red pepper or tomato halves.

Yield: 6 to 8 servings

Plimouth Plantation Boiled Salad

This recipe dates back to the seventeenth century, when cooks thought of any vegetable—whether cooked or uncooked—as a salad, or "sallet." The sweet-and-sour side dish is a standard at the seasonal dinners held at Plimouth Plantation, in Massachusetts.

1 firm head of cabbage (about 2 lb)
½ tsp salt (or more)
½ cup currants

1 tbsp brown sugar
¼ cup unsalted butter
⅓ cup vinegar (white or cider)

Separate cabbage leaves, trimming away any shriveled outer leaves, and cut the heart into 4 pieces. Fill a large saucepan one-quarter full with water, adding ½ teaspoon of salt to each pint. Bring water to a boil.

Add cabbage, cover and cook at medium heat until tender, about 10 minutes. Remove from heat and drain off liquid. While cabbage is still in the pot, chop it well with a spoon, and add currants, brown sugar, butter, and vinegar. Return to heat and gently boil mixture for 5 minutes.

Sprinkle with additional brown sugar and serve.

Yield: 6 to 8 servings

New England Cranberry Vinaigrette

The Inn of the Golden Ox, in Brewster, Massachusetts, takes a break from traditional cranberry relishes with this tangy cranberry vinaigrette. Innkeeper Eileen Gibson serves it with a three-greens salad of Boston lettuce, Romaine lettuce, and spinach, garnished with red onion and freshly chopped cranberries marinated in cranberry vinegar.

2 egg yolks
2 tbsp shallots, finely diced
6 oz cranberry vinegar
½ cup fresh orange juice
2 tbsp fresh lemon juice

1 pt soy oil
½ cup cranberries (preferably fresh; if using frozen, ¼ cup)
2 tbsp grenadine

In large stainless steel bowl, combine egg yolks, shallots, cranberry vinegar, orange juice, and lemon juice. Whisk lightly to begin to incorporate ingredients. Continue whisking and drizzle in oil in a steady stream until fully incorporated. Add cranberries and grenadine for color as desired. The Inn favors a light peach color.

Serve with spinach, escarole, or any hearty greens.

Yield: 3 cups dressing

Cranberries Braised in Red Wine

At the Benn Conger Inn, located along the Finger Lakes in northern New York State, Thanksgiving is a time for enjoying the invigorating pleasures of an early winter and the quiet joys of an elegant holiday feast. Cranberries Braised in Red Wine is but one of the special touches that combine tradition and contemporary cuisine. The innkeeper, Mark Bloom, suggests that you prepare this dish a day or two before the holiday to allow the flavors to blend and intensify.

1 16-oz bag fresh cranberries　　　　　*peel of 1 orange, finely chopped*
1 cup red wine　　　　　　　　　　　　*1 cinnamon stick*
1 ½ cups sugar

Sort through cranberries and discard any soft or unripe ones. Bring wine and sugar to a boil in a saucepan and add all other ingredients. Cover partially and reduce heat to medium. Cook until cranberries have burst and sauce is slightly thickened, about 15 to 20 minutes. Cool to room temperature and serve.

Yield: 6 to 8 servings

Grandmother Galatha Sterner's Thanksgiving Mustard Onions

Galatha Comstock Sterner's Mustard Onions have been passed along over three generations of mothers and daughters. This side dish brings back the best in family eating. Rich, creamy, and redolent of mustard and horseradish, the onions add bite and tang to more subdued holiday flavors.

2 lb small white boiling　　　　　　　*1 tsp prepared mustard*
　onions, peeled and whole,　　　　　　*1 tsp prepared horseradish*
　or yellow onions, peeled and sliced　　*or horseradish-flavored mustard*
½ tsp salt　　　　　　　　　　　　　　*½ cup milk*
1 to 1 ½ tbsp unsalted　　　　　　　　*½ cup water*
　butter or shortening　　　　　　　　　*salt and pepper to taste*
1 ½ tbsp all-purpose flour

Preheat oven to 350°.

Add onions to salted water, almost to cover, and simmer for about 10 minutes. Meanwhile, over medium heat, melt butter in a small saucepan and stir in flour to form a paste. Stir in the mustard and horseradish, then gradually add the milk and water, stirring constantly. Cook this mixture until thickened. Season with salt and pepper to taste, and remove from heat.

Drain onions and place them in ungreased ovenproof casserole. Pour sauce over the onions, cover, and bake for 15 to 20 minutes. To give the dish a little color, remove the lid for the last 10 minutes of cooking.

Yield: 6 servings

Grandma Bost's Candied Yams

In a rambling white farmhouse atop a hill in Mount Pleasant, North Carolina, Grandma Bost has been concocting her special blend of yams, raisins, and marshmallows for over 50 years. For southern cooks, yams are a traditional Sunday dish, not just a holiday treat. But on Thanksgiving, when Grandma Bost's six children, 15 grandchildren, and three great-grandchildren come to call, she admits that the occasion calls for a few extra raisins and an extra pinch of love.

3 medium sweet potatoes (about 2 lb)   *½ tsp cinnamon*
2 tbsp butter   *⅓ cup maple syrup, honey, or molasses*
⅓ cup raisins   *2 tbsp lemon juice or orange juice*
pinch of salt   *½ to ¾ cup miniature marshmallows*

Preheat oven to 350°.

In large pot of boiling water, cook sweet potatoes until tender, about 40 minutes. When sweet potatoes have cooled, peel them and cut into ½-inch slices. Place in baking dish, dot with butter and sprinkle with raisins. Top with salt, cinnamon, and maple syrup, honey, or molasses. Drizzle with juice and bake for 25 minutes. Remove from oven, top with marshmallows, and bake for an additional 5 minutes, until marshmallows have browned. Serve hot.

Yield: 4 to 6 servings

Sweet Taters and Apples

This traditional recipe hails from the Ozarks, where hearty cooking and lots of it is a way of life. No Thanksgiving would be complete without this version of the perfect sweet potato casserole, heady with the scent of nutmeg and fresh apples.

6 medium sweet potatoes or yams
6 medium cooking apples
½ cup melted butter

⅓ cup light brown sugar
½ teaspoon ground nutmeg

Preheat oven to 400°.

Bake the sweet potatoes in their skins for 1 hour or until tender. Remove from heat and reduce oven to 350°. When sweet potatoes are cool enough to handle, peel and cut into ¼- to ½-inch slices. Peel, core, and slice the apples. Layer sliced potatoes and apples alternately in a 9″ × 9″ × 2″ baking dish, scattering melted butter, brown sugar, and nutmeg over each layer. Cover with foil and bake 30 to 35 minutes until bubbly.

Yield: 6 servings

Ancient New England Standing Dish of Pompions

Pumpkins, or as they were called in old New England, pompions, were a saving grace to the new settlers. They grew easily and plentifully in the region, and naturally became a staple of the settlers' diet. As a 1630 folksong, "The Forefather's Song," announces:

> *For pottage and puddings and custards and pies*
> *Our pumpkins and parsnips are common supplies;*
> *We have pumpkin at morning and pumpkin at noon,*
> *If it was not for pumpkin, we should be undone.*

According to Plimouth Plantation, this is one of the few detailed New England recipes that has survived. It was adapted by the Plantation from a recipe in a 1672 cookbook by John Josselyn called *New England Verites Discovered*. Allow plenty of time to cook this dish, for it must be done very slowly.

8 cups peeled diced pumpkin   ⅓ cup brown sugar
¼ cup water   ¼ tsp ground ginger
2 tbsp butter   ¼ tsp cinnamon
2 tbsp vinegar   salt to taste

Place 2 cups pumpkin and ¼ cup water into a pot and cook gently over low heat until pumpkin softens, about 10 minutes. Gradually add the rest of the pumpkin and continue cooking until the entire mixture is tender and pumpkin retains much of its form, about 20 to 30 minutes. The mixture should resemble stewed apples.

Remove from heat and add butter, vinegar, brown sugar, and spices. Stir gently and serve immediately.

Yield: 6 to 8 servings

Classic Fluffy Mashed Potatoes

Now that you have created the perfect giblet gravy, the only way to showcase it is to prepare the perfect mashed potatoes. For many people, mashed potatoes are the reason gravy was invented. This is a recipe for the real thing, just like Grandma used to make. Don't even think about using a food processor; it will turn the potatoes into mush. This dish was meant to be prepared the old-fashioned way—by hand.

6 medium potatoes   6 tbsp butter (1 tbsp for garnish)
⅔ cup milk, warmed   salt and pepper to taste

Peel the potatoes and cut into large chunks. Place in large saucepan of water and boil until tender, about 15 minutes. Drain potatoes and return to very low heat. Add half the milk and 5 tbsp butter. Mash with a potato masher to remove lumps, then whip with fork until potatoes are fluffy. Add remaining milk, if necessary, plus salt and pepper. Top with butter and serve immediately.

Yield: 4 to 6 servings

NOTE: For a heartier version of this classic, mix ½ cup chopped onion sautéed in butter into the potatoes just before serving.

Marilyn's Acorn Squash Mash

Squash is the traditional harvest vegetable, and no respectable Thanksgiving table would be complete without it. In this delectable recipe, pure maple syrup makes all the difference. This dish can be made two to three days ahead. It also freezes well.

3 medium acorn squash   4 tbsp butter, softened
¼ cup cream or milk   ¼ tsp ground nutmeg, if desired
¼ cup maple syrup   salt to taste

Preheat oven to 400°.

Prick squash with fork. Place directly on oven rack and bake until soft, about 1 to 1¼ hours. Let cool slightly; peel and seed as soon as squash is cool enough to handle. (This allows steam to escape, preventing a watery dish.) Puree until smooth in blender or food processor fitted with steel blade. Add other ingredients until blended completely.

    Serve immediately, or keep warm in covered saucepan on stove top over very low heat, or heat in buttered casserole in a 350° oven for 30 minutes.

Yield: 6 to 8 servings

Candied Apple Wedges

Anyone who thinks candied apples are a thing of the past has only to visit Schumacher's New Prague Hotel, in New Prague, Minnesota, at holiday time. Golden, glazed apples in abundance surround the goose, providing a sweet counterpart to the Czechoslovakian Dressing (p. 41). Executive chef John Schumacher says that preparing the candied apples late in the day fills the house with an inviting holiday scent.

6 to 8 apples, Jonathan or Winesap   1 cup brown sugar
2 tbsp butter   pinch of salt

Core apples and slice into wedges. Do not peel. In a frying pan, dissolve brown sugar in butter. Add apples and a pinch of salt. Cook uncovered on very low heat for about 1 hour, turning frequently. Serve immediately.

Yield: 6 to 8 servings

Breads and Biscuits

Grandma Conner's Baking Powder Biscuits

With Thanksgiving stuffings, side dishes, and relishes, it may seem easy to neglect the breads—until you are left with a plate of luscious turkey gravy and you need a slice or a biscuit to collect it. These biscuits are simple, foolproof, and delicious. Grandma Conner created them nearly 50 years ago in Guildford, Maine, to accompany her husband's oyster stew. They are ideal for Thanksgiving sauces, jellies, and relishes.

2 ½ cups all-purpose flour	¾ tsp salt
2 ½ tbsp cream of tartar	2 tbsp shortening
1 ¼ tsp baking soda	¾ cup milk

Preheat oven to 425°.

In large mixing bowl, sift together flour, cream of tartar, baking soda, and salt. Work shortening into the mixture, first using a wooden spoon, then your fingers, or pastry blender, fork, or two knives. Stir in enough milk to make the dough very moist but not sticky—the secret to moist, puffy biscuits.

Turn dough out onto a very lightly floured board. Knead it up to 10 turns and then pat it into a flat circle. With a floured rolling pin, roll out the dough to ½-inch thickness. Cut into biscuits with a lightly floured 2-inch round cutter or glass. For crispy-crust biscuits, place biscuits about 1 inch apart on an ungreased baking sheet, closer together for soft-crust biscuits. Prick the top of the biscuits with a fork. Bake for 10 to 12 minutes, until golden brown. Remove from the sheet immediately and serve hot.

NOTE: To make drop biscuits, add a few more tablespoons of milk to the dough and drop by teaspoonfuls onto a greased baking sheet.

Yield: 16 biscuits

Plimouth Plantation Cornbread Biscuits

This year, instead of restricting your holiday cornbread to a Thanksgiving stuffing, feature it in a holiday biscuit. This recipe is a standard at Plimouth Plantation celebrations all year round, and with good reason—it is simple, healthful, and satisfying.

1 cup cornmeal   1 ½ cups whole wheat flour
4 cups water   1 tsp salt

Preheat oven to 375°.

Place the cornmeal and water in a large pot and bring to a boil. Lower heat to simmer and cook, stirring occasionally, until very thick, about ½ hour. Blend the whole wheat flour and salt into the cooked cornmeal until well mixed. With hands or ½-cup measure, place ½-cup-sized biscuit-shaped mounds onto ungreased cookie sheet. Press down each mound slightly with measuring cup or fork. Bake for 15 minutes; then turn cornbreads over and bake an additional 10 minutes.

Yield: 36 biscuits

Myrtle Orloff's Appleanna Bread

Grandma Myrtle Orloff has been many things in her life: a seamstress, photographer, golfer, and even the first woman car salesperson. Today, she lives in Cambridge, Massachusetts, where she works as a volunteer for local hospitals. Her flavorful Appleanna Bread has been rousing her household on the holidays for more than four decades.

½ cup plus 1 tbsp shortening
1½ cups sugar
2 large eggs, at room temperature, lightly beaten
2 cups all-purpose flour
1 tsp baking soda
1 tsp baking powder

1 tsp cinnamon, ground
1 tsp salt
2 very ripe bananas, peeled and mashed
2 cups apples, peeled, cored, and finely chopped
1 tsp vanilla extract

Preheat the oven to 350°. With 1 tablespoon of shortening, grease and flour a 9″ loaf pan.

Cream together shortening and sugar until light; add eggs. Sift together flour, baking soda, baking powder, cinnamon, and salt; beat together with shortening mixture. Stir in mashed bananas, apples, and vanilla extract. Pour the batter into prepared pan and bake for 1 hour, or until a knife inserted in the middle comes out clean.

Yield: 1 loaf

Desserts and Sweet Treats

Marlborough Pudding

Rich and fragrant, Marlborough Pudding was one of the stars of the early nineteenth-century Thanksgiving feast. This recipe from the *Old Sturbridge Village Cookbook* is the lush finale at the historic Massachusetts village's Thanksgiving celebration. Serve it with freshly whipped cream and grated nutmeg.

puff pastry for 8-inch deep-dish pie
juice and peel of 1 lemon
  (omit if using applesauce)
2 large fresh apples or 1 cup applesauce

1 cup sugar
  (use only ⅓ cup if using applesauce)
3 eggs
½ cup butter

Preheat oven to 400°.

PUFF PASTRY

1 cup butter
1 ¾ cups sifted whole wheat flour

¼ cup cold water

Blend ⅓ cup butter and 1 cup flour. Gradually add ¼ cup cold water. Roll out onto a floured board. Dot with half the remaining butter, sprinkle with ⅜ cup of remaining flour (dusting some on rolling pin), and roll up like a jelly roll. Roll out and repeat process with remaining flour and butter.

   Line pie plate with pastry.

FILLING

Squeeze lemon and grate peel into large bowl. Grate apples into lemon juice and toss to coat apples to prevent darkening. Pour sugar over fruit and mix well. In separate bowl, beat eggs until light. Cream butter until soft and add eggs, blending well. Stir butter and egg mixture into sweetened fruit and spoon into pie shell. Bake 15 minutes, then reduce heat to 350° and bake for an additional 45 minutes, or until a knife inserted in the center comes out clean. Cool before serving.

Yield: 1 deep-dish pie

Reprinted with permission from *Old Sturbridge Village Cookbook: Authentic Early American Recipes for the Modern Kitchen*, edited by Caroline Sloat, © 1984, published by The Globe Pequot Press, Chester, CT 06412.

Shaker Date-Pecan Pudding

Pies and puddings were traditional desserts in the early American household. Every family had its favorite—pumpkin, raisin, Indian. The Shakers prepared many types of puddings, but saved the date-pecan creation for such special occasions as Thanksgiving.

1 cup dates, chopped   *1 tsp baking powder*
1 cup pecan pieces   *2 eggs*
⅔ cup sugar   *¼ cup cream*
1 tbsp flour   *½ tsp vanilla*

Preheat oven to 350°.

Mix dates, pecans, sugar, flour, and baking powder by hand. Beat eggs well in a separate bowl. Add cream and vanilla to eggs and mix lightly with a fork. Add to date-and-nut mixture. Turn into buttered casserole. The mixture should half-fill the casserole. Place casserole into large pan and partially fill pan (not casserole) with water. Bake for about 45 minutes, until crust forms. Serve warm or cold with heavy cream or your favorite vanilla custard sauce.

Yield: 6-8 servings

Mama Boyd's Sweet Potato Pie

Mama Boyd had a 700-acre farm in Orangeburg, South Carolina, way back off the main road, where the earth is a beautiful orange. She ran a small country store near one of those roads, where she sold her family's homegrown chickens, corn, homemade sausages, canned goods, and this sweet potato pie. Rich, spicy, and flavorful, it is as popular a Thanksgiving dessert in the South as pumpkin pie is in the North. Freshly grated ginger and nutmeg make the pie even more appealing.

PIE CRUST FOR SINGLE-CRUST PIE

8-INCH SHELL

1 cup plus 2 tbsp flour   *⅓ cup shortening*
¼ tsp salt   *2-3 tbsp cold water*

9-INCH SHELL

1 ½ cups flour   *⅓ cup shortening*
¼ tsp salt   *3-4 tbsp cold water*

Mix the flour and salt. Cut in the shortening with a pastry blender, two knives, or food processor. Combine lightly until the mixture resembles coarse meal. Sprinkle water over the flour mixture, a tablespoon at a time, and mix lightly with a fork, using only enough water so that the pastry will hold together when pressed gently into a ball.

FILLING

1 ½ cups (about 4 medium)   *½ tsp ground ginger*
  sweet potatoes or yams,   *½ tsp grated nutmeg*
  cooked and mashed   *¼ tsp ground cloves*
2 tbsp unsalted butter   *½ tsp salt*
  or shortening, melted   *2 large eggs, beaten*
1 tsp grated orange or   *1 ½ cups milk, scalded*
  lemon peel   *1 cup heavy cream*
½ cup brown sugar, firmly packed *1 tbsp white sugar*
1 tbsp ground cinnamon   *2 tbsp chopped pecans*

Preheat oven to 450°.

Place sweet potatoes or yams in a large bowl and stir in the melted butter and grated orange or lemon peel. Combine brown sugar, cinnamon, ginger, nutmeg, cloves, and salt, and beat into the sweet potato mixture. Gradually beat in the eggs. Stir in the scalded milk, blending well. Pour into the prepared pastry shell.

Bake for 10 minutes, then reduce the temperature to 350° and bake for an additional 30 to 35 minutes, or until a knife comes out clean when inserted halfway between the center and the edge of the filling.

Cool the pie on a wire rack. When ready to serve, whip the cream with the sugar and spread it over the pie. Sprinkle the top with chopped pecans.

Yield: 1 pie

Cranberry Pie

A traditional favorite from the *Old Sturbridge Village Cookbook*, this simple Thanksgiving dessert is but one of the array of pies at the annual nineteenth-century Thanksgiving celebration at the historical community.

1 9-inch pie shell (p. 62)	*2-3 cups brown sugar*
1 lb whole cranberries,	*2 cups water*
washed and sorted	*¼ tsp nutmeg or cinnamon*

Preheat oven to 350°.

In large saucepan, combine cranberries, 2 cups brown sugar, and water. Simmer until cranberries pop and syrup has thickened, about 10 minutes. Add spices and taste. Add sugar if mixture seems too tart.

Spoon mixture into pie shell and bake for 30 minutes.

Yield: 1 pie

Reprinted with permission from *Old Sturbridge Village Cookbook: Authentic Early American Recipes for the Modern Kitchen*, edited by Caroline Sloat, © 1984, published by The Globe Pequot Press, Chester, CT 06412.

> *''I don't think a really good pie can be made without a*
> *dozen or so children peeking over your shoulder as you stoop*
> *to look in at it every little while.''*
> —John Gould

Pumpkin-Pecan Tart

Northern and southern fancies unite in this pumpkin-pecan delicacy from Benn Conger Inn, in Groton, New York. Serve the tart with freshly whipped cream. Don't skimp on the pecans!

1 9-inch pie shell (p. 62)	*¼ tsp nutmeg*
1 cup pecans, coarsely chopped	*½ tsp ginger*
½ cup brown sugar	*1 tsp cinnamon*
¼ tsp salt	*¼ tsp cloves*
3 tbsp butter, melted	*½ tsp salt*
1 cup mashed pumpkin	*½ cup heavy cream*
2 eggs	*½ cup half-and-half*

Preheat oven to 350°.

Combine pecans coarsely with brown sugar, salt, and butter, and mix well. Roll out pie dough and fit into 9-inch open tart pan. Spread pecan mix evenly on bottom. Mix all other ingredients together and pour into tart shell. Bake for about 1 hour or until knife inserted in pie comes out clean.

Yield: 1 pie

Pecan Pie

Thanksgiving family-style dinner at The Smith House, in Dahlonega, Georgia, wouldn't be the same without trays of delectable pecan pie. This recipe, from The Smith House's cookbook, *The Boarding House Reach Cookbook,* is everything the Southern specialty should be: buttery, nutty, and fragrant with brandy.

1 9-inch pie shell (p. 62)	*½ cup dark corn syrup*
3 eggs	*½ cup whipping cream*
1 cup sugar	*1 tsp vanilla*
½ tsp salt	*¼ cup brandy*
2 tbsp butter, melted	*1 cup pecan halves*

Preheat oven to 375°.

In a small mixer bowl, beat eggs, sugar, salt, butter, corn syrup, and cream. Stir in vanilla, brandy, and pecans. Pour into pie shell. Bake 40 to 50 minutes, or until filling is set and pastry is golden brown. Cool before serving.

Yield: 1 pie

Baked Apples in Caramel Sauce

Baked apples and caramel apples are favorite harvest-time treats. Now they come together in another tempting Thanksgiving dessert from Carter House Bed and Breakfast Inn, in Eureka, California. Serve with whipped cream and fresh mint sprigs (if possible) for a continental touch.

4 Granny Smith apples   *¾ cup granulated sugar*
½ cup unsalted butter, melted

CARAMEL SAUCE

⅔ cup sugar   *1 tbsp butter*
3 tbsp cold water   *1 tsp vanilla*
2 tbsp hot water   *whipped cream (for garnish)*
¾ cup cream   *fresh mint leaves (for garnish)*

Preheat broiler.

Peel and core the apples, cut them in half, and lightly score the tops. Roll each apple half in melted butter, then in sugar. Cover a baking sheet with aluminum foil, and place apples on foil. Broil the apples for about 10 minutes, or until the tops are browned. Remove the baking sheet from broiler and set aside.

In heavy saucepan, combine the sugar and the cold water. Bring the mixture to a boil, stirring constantly. When the mixture begins to brown, remove the saucepan from the heat. Add the hot water carefully, as the mixture may splatter. Quickly add the cream, stirring constantly. Return the pan to a medium low heat and whisk in the butter and add the vanilla.

Place the apple halves on dessert or salad plates. Drizzle with caramel sauce and garnish with whipped cream and mint sprigs.

Yield: 8 servings

Furmenty

Puddings and custards were a staple in the early American diet, and Furmenty was a favorite at harvest time. This recipe from Plimouth Plantation is based on the Furmenty recipes that were prepared in Plymouth in the 1620s.

1 qt water	*⅛ tsp ground mace*
1 cup cracked wheat	*½ tsp cinnamon*
¾ cup milk	*¼ cup brown sugar*
½ cup heavy cream	*2 egg yolks*
½ tsp salt	*additional brown sugar (for garnish)*

In large pot, bring water to a boil and add wheat. Lower heat to simmer, cover, and continue to cook for 30 minutes or until soft. Drain off all water and add milk, cream, mace, cinnamon, and brown sugar. Continue to simmer, stirring occasionally, until most of the liquid is absorbed, about 20 to 30 minutes. In a small bowl, beat the egg yolks and slowly stir ½ cup of the wheat mixture into the yolks. Stir the yolk mixture into the pot, and continue cooking for another 5 minutes, stirring frequently. Serve sprinkled with brown sugar.

Yield: 8 servings

(Picture collection, the Branch Libraries, the New York Public Library)

After-Dinner Drinks

Mulled Cider

Life at the Arkansas Territorial Restoration, in Little Rock, is just the way it was in the early nineteenth century, when Arkansas was young, from the impressively restored homesteads to the old-fashioned holiday meals. No holiday feast, no matter how lavish, would be complete without hot mulled cider. This bracing dinner finale is based on an old recipe that dates back to territorial days.

2 sticks cinnamon
12 whole cloves
2 tsp whole allspice

1 gal apple cider
1 cup light brown sugar, firmly packed
1 lemon, thinly sliced

Tie cinnamon sticks, cloves, and allspice in a small cheesecloth bag. Pour cider into a large, heavy enamel kettle, then add bag of spices and brown sugar. Simmer, uncovered, for 15 minutes. Remove the bag of spices. Pour cider into a metal or heatproof punch bowl, float lemon slices on top, and serve hot.

Yield: 12 servings

Hot Buttered Rum

While it is a New England custom to present this recipe in individual servings, you may of course multiply it to match your crowd—or your thirst. Be warned, however: this drink packs a wallop, especially at the end of a hectic Thanksgiving Day.

1 cup water or apple cider
1 tsp powdered sugar
¼ cup dark rum

1 tbsp unsalted butter
1 stick cinnamon
freshly grated nutmeg

Bring water or cider to boil. Add sugar and rum. Stir well and remove from flame. Mix in butter and serve in warmed mugs. Serve with cinnamon stick or sprinkle with freshly grated nutmeg.

Yield: 1 serving

Plimouth Plantation White Ipocras

Ipocras is a traditional early American wine recipe—strong, spicy, full-bodied. It was reserved for special occasions. It was named after Hippocrates (father of the Hippocratic oath) because the bag of spices that flavored the wine, like the ancient physician's bag of herbs, seemed to work magic. Plimouth Plantation serves Ipocras at all its seasonal events.

1 bottle (⅘ quart) white wine
½ cup sugar
4 cloves

4 peppercorns
1 2-inch stick cinnamon
1 2-inch piece fresh (green) ginger

Pour wine into a large bowl. Add sugar and stir until dissolved. Bruise the cloves and peppercorns with a spice press or fork and add to the wine with the cinnamon and ginger. Cover and refrigerate for at least 24 hours. Strain liquid through a jelly bag or clean white cloth before serving.

Yield: 6 to 8 servings

Thanksgiving
Leftover Specialties

Leftovers

Thanksgiving has been over
at least a week or two,
but we're still all eating turkey,
turkey salad, turkey stew,
turkey puffs and turkey pudding,
turkey patties, turkey pies,
turkey bisque and turkey burgers,
turkey fritters, turkey fries.

For lunch our mother made us
turkey slices on a stick,
there'll be turkey tarts for supper,
all this turkey makes me sick.

For tomorrow she's preparing
turkey dumplings stuffed with peas,
oh I never thought I'd say this—
"Mother! No more turkey...PLEASE!"

—*Jack Prelutsky,* It's Thanksgiving, *1982*

Thanksgiving Turkey-Pomegranate Salad

Turkey, fresh apple, pineapple, and almonds come together in this holiday specialty on the Thanksgiving weekend. It is one of the most popular creations of the Patchwork Quilt Country Inn, of Middlebury, Indiana. For marvelous leftover sandwiches, team this fruity salad with a full-bodied bread, such as the cornmeal-based Millbrook Anadama Bread (p. 72) or Whole Wheat Molasses Bread (p. 73).

1 cup pineapple bits, drained
3 cups diced cooked turkey
1 cup celery, sliced on the slant
1 cup diced apples (Rome, Winesap,
 or any red-skinned variety)

½ cup pomegranate seeds
½ cup toasted slivered almonds
1 cup mayonnaise
¼ cup sour cream
¼ cup pineapple juice

Toss pineapple in large bowl with turkey, celery, apple, pomegranate seeds, and almonds. In separate bowl, combine mayonnaise, sour cream, and pineapple juice. Toss dressing with turkey mix in the larger bowl. Garnish with additional pomegranate seeds and toasted almonds.

Yield: 8 servings

Chinese Turkey Salad

If you want a break from tradition, prepare this Oriental-style turkey salad. Serve it with leftovers at a Colonial-Chinese Day-After-Thanksgiving Brunch.

2 cups julienned cooked turkey
2 cups cooked rice, cooled
2 cups torn fresh spinach
1 medium tomato, diced
½ cup pea pods, cut into
 1-inch pieces
1 can (8 oz) water chestnuts, drained

¼ cup condensed beef broth
¼ cup lemon juice
1 tbsp soy sauce
1 tbsp vegetable or corn oil
1-2 tbsp peanut butter (optional)
1 tbsp sugar
6 slices bacon, cooked and crumbled

In large bowl, combine turkey, rice, spinach, tomato, pea pods, and water chestnuts. In small saucepan, combine beef broth, lemon juice, soy sauce, oil, peanut butter, and sugar. Heat until peanut butter melts and sugar dissolves. Cool. Pour over turkey mixture; toss gently. Chill 1 hour. Garnish with bacon and serve.

Yield: 6 servings, 1 cup each

Garden-Patch Turkey Stew with Dumplings

When it's Saturday and the turkey is still staring at you from a refrigerator shelf, the only response is soup. Something easy to make, fresh-tasting, and easily adaptable to whatever else you have on hand—that's what you want. Garden-Patch Turkey Stew fills the bill. With its fresh dumplings and wealth of vegetables, it gives the weekend an original twist.

1 medium onion, sliced	*2 13¾-oz cans chicken broth*
2 ribs celery, sliced	*1 cup water*
1 16-oz can tomatoes, undrained	*2 tsp sugar*
2 tbsp butter or margarine	*1½ tsp marjoram leaves*
3 cups cubed cooked turkey	*1 tsp salt*
2 cups coarsely chopped cabbage	*2 cups buttermilk baking mix*
1 15½-oz can kidney beans, undrained	*⅔ cup milk*

In Dutch oven or large saucepan, sauté onion and celery in butter until crisp-tender. Cut up tomatoes and save juice. Add turkey, cabbage, tomatoes and juice, beans, broth, water, sugar, marjoram, and salt. Cover and simmer 25 minutes, or until cabbage is tender. Stir together baking mix and milk until soft dough is formed. Drop by spoonfuls onto boiling stew to make 12 dumplings. Cover and simmer 15 minutes.

Yield: 6-8 servings

Turkey Barley Chowder

Nothing soothes the soul (and makes for an easy meal) like a cup of soup. With leftover Chestnut Stuffing (p. 43) and a tossed salad dressed with New England Cranberry Vinaigrette (p. 51), it makes a satisfying meal that fondly recalls the spirit of the holiday meal.

2 cups diced cooked turkey	*1 cup water*
2 13¾-oz cans chicken broth	*1½ tbsp sugar*
1 15-oz can tomato sauce with	*¼ tsp cloves*
tomato bits	*½ cup half-and-half*
¼ cup medium pearl barley	*1 tbsp sherry*
1 medium onion, sliced thin	*1 tbsp chopped fresh parsley*

Combine turkey, broth, tomato sauce, barley, onion, water, sugar, and cloves in large saucepan. Cover and simmer, stirring occasionally, for 1 hour, or until barley is tender. Stir in half-and-half and sherry. Heat to serving temperature; do not boil. Garnish with parsley.

Yield: 6 to 8 servings

Millbrook Anadama Bread

This traditional bread from the Millbrook Lodge, in Waitsfield, Vermont, is based on an old New England recipe with a colorful history. During the whaling era, there was a sea captain with a wife named Anna. She was an uninspired cook whose only dish was cornmeal mush. In anger and frustration, the captain would storm around his ship, ranting, ''Anna, damn her, the laziest cook alive!''

On the day after Thanksgiving, innkeeper Joan Gorman features the bread in her Open-Faced Hot Turkey Anadama Bread Sandwich, which has become a post-holiday tradition at the Lodge. To prepare it, simply pile a thick slice of untoasted Anadama Bread with warmed leftover stuffing, cold turkey, and hot gravy. Devour to your heart's content!

1 cup yellow cornmeal (any grind)	*4 tsp salt*
4 cups boiling water	*2 packages dry yeast,*
2 tbsp unsalted butter	*dissolved in 1 cup lukewarm water*
1 cup molasses (light or dark)	*9 cups white flour*

Grease 4 loaf pans (8½″ × 4½″) and set aside.

Place cornmeal in large ceramic bowl; pour in boiling water, add butter in pieces, and stir until there are no lumps of cornmeal and butter is melted. Let mixture stand for 30 minutes.

Stir in molasses and salt. Dissolve yeast in lukewarm water and stir into cornmeal mixture. Add flour all at once. Stir to wet flour. Mix with your hands only until flour is absorbed. Do not overmix; it will cause the bread to become dense. Dough will be very sticky—this is normal.

Spoon dough into the greased loaf pans, cover with a cloth, and set in a warm place to rise. Let rise until double in bulk.

Preheat oven to 350°.

Bake for 45 minutes. Do not overbake. Remove from oven and turn out of pans immediately onto rack to cool. Do not cut bread until it is completely cool.

Yield: 4 loaves

Whole Wheat Molasses Bread

Simple, healthy Whole Wheat Molasses Bread should provide a breath of fresh air after the excesses of the Thanksgiving feast. This staple, from the Benn Conger Inn, in Groton, New York, is a perfect sandwich-mate for any type of fowl or game. No matter how you slice it, it's a marvelous way to go cold turkey!

2 cups white flour	*1 tsp dry yeast*
2½ cups whole wheat flour	*1½ cups warm water*
1 tsp salt	*½ cup molasses*

Preheat oven to 175°.

Mix flours and salt in metal bowl and put in warm oven until mixture is slightly warm. Mix yeast and ½ cup warm water, let proof for five minutes. Add molasses to yeast and water mix. Take flour mixture from oven; add yeast and mix warm water (up to 1 cup) to make a slightly wet and sticky dough. Put directly into 2 buttered 9-inch bread pans. Let rise 1½ hours until the dough is at the top of the pans. Meanwhile, heat oven to 350°. Bake 45 minutes to an hour, or until the bread is dark brown and sounds hollow when tapped. Serve warm with plenty of unsalted butter.

Yield: 2 loaves

THANKSGIVING STORIES AND POEMS

"While John Inglefield and his family were sitting round the hearth with the shadows dancing behind them on the wall, the outer door was opened, and a light footstep came along the passage. The latch of the inner door was lifted by some familiar hand, and a young girl came in, wearing a cloak and hood, which she took off and laid on the table beneath the looking-glass. Then, after gazing a moment at the fireside circle, she approached, and took the seat at John Inglefield's right hand, as if it had been reserved on purpose for her."

—Nathaniel Hawthorne,
"John Inglefield's Thanksgiving," 1840

"Sharing a Thanksgiving Story," artist unknown (Culver Pictures)

We experience an array of emotions at holiday time, each unique to our time, place, and condition. Stories and poems have captured such human experiences and have preserved them for us. Through the ages, people have depended upon writers and artists to distill the essence of human experience into a form that could be relived time and time again. When we read a great story or poem, we not only re-experience the writer's feeling and thought at the time of its conception, but we learn something about our own life as well.

Reading something well written deepens us, and we emerge from the words changed, ready to be changed again. In this collection of Thanksgiving stories and poems, you will find a wide range of recollections from the masters—from the simple gratitude of Ralph Waldo Emerson's classic poem, "We Thank Thee," to the grandeur of Hezekiah Butterworth's "The Thanksgiving in Boston Harbor" to the darker side of relationships in Nathaniel Hawthorne's "John Inglefield's Thanksgiving." You will experience a variety of historical visions as well: Boston Harbor in 1631, a quiet—or almost quiet—dinner table in nineteenth-century New England, and New York's Union Square at the turn of the twentieth century. Each of these writings will take you into a new and different world.

Share these tales and poems by reading them aloud to your family and friends: it will make for a Thanksgiving you cannot forget.

(Picture collection, the Branch Libraries, the New York Public Library)

John Inglefield's Thanksgiving

On the evening of Thanksgiving Day, John Inglefield, the blacksmith, sat in his elbow-chair, among those who had been keeping festival at his board. Being the central figure of the domestic circle, the fire threw its strongest light on his massive and sturdy frame, reddening his rough visage, so that it looked like the head of an iron statue, all aglow, from his own forge, and with its features rudely fashioned on his own anvil. At John Inglefield's right hand was an empty chair. The other places around the hearth were filled by the members of the family, who all sat quietly, while, with a semblance of fantastic merriment, their shadows danced on the wall behind them. One of the group was John Inglefield's son, who had been bred at college, and was now a student of theology at Andover. There was also a daughter of sixteen, whom nobody could look at without thinking of a rosebud almost blossomed. The only other person at the fireside was Robert Moore, formerly an apprentice of the blacksmith, but now his journeyman, and who seemed more like an own son of John Inglefield than did the pale and slender student.

Only these four had kept New England's festival beneath that roof. The vacant chair at John Inglefield's right hand was in memory of his wife, whom death had snatched from him since the previous Thanksgiving. With a feeling that few would have looked for in his rough nature, the bereaved husband had himself set the chair in its place next his own; and often did his eye glance hitherward, as if he deemed it possible that the cold grave might send back its tenant to the cheerful fireside, at least for that one evening. Thus did he cherish the grief that was dear to him. But there was another grief which he would fain have torn from his heart; or, since that could never be, have buried it too deep for others to behold, or for his own remembrance. Within the past year another member of his household had gone from him, but not to the grave. Yet they kept no vacant chair for her.

While John Inglefield and his family were sitting round the hearth with the shadows dancing behind them on the wall, the outer door was opened, and a light footstep came along the passage. The latch of the inner door was lifted by some familiar hand, and a young girl came in, wearing a cloak and hood, which she took off and laid on the table beneath the looking-glass. Then, after gazing a moment at the fireside circle, she approached, and took the seat at John Inglefield's right hand, as if it had been reserved on purpose for her.

"Here I am, at last, father," she said. "You ate your Thanksgiving dinner without me, but I have come back to spend the evening with you."

Yes, it was Prudence Inglefield. She wore the same neat and maidenly attire which she had been accustomed to put on when the household work was over for the day, and her hair was parted from her brow, in the simple and modest fashion that became her best of all. If her cheek might otherwise have been pale, yet the glow of the fire suffused it with a healthful bloom. If she had spent the many months of her absence in guilt and infamy, yet they seemed to have left no traces on her gentle aspect. She could not have looked less altered, had she merely stepped away from her father's fireside for half an hour, and returned while the blaze was quivering upwards from the same brands that were burning at her departure. And to John Inglefield she was the very image of his buried wife, such as he remembered on the first Thanksgiving which they had passed under their own roof. Therefore, though naturally a stern and rugged man, he could not speak unkindly to his sinful child, nor yet could he take her to his bosom.

"You are welcome home, Prudence," said he, glancing sideways at her, and his voice faltered. "Your mother would have rejoiced to see you, but she has been gone from us these four months."

"I know, father, I know it," replied Prudence, quickly. "And yet, when I first came in, my eyes were so dazzled by the firelight that she seemed to be sitting in this very chair."

By this time, the other members of the family had begun to recover from their surprise, and became sensible that it was no ghost from the grave, nor vision of their vivid recollections, but Prudence, her own self. Her brother was the next that greeted her. He advanced and held out his hand affectionately, as a brother should; yet not entirely like a brother, for, with all his kindness, he was still a clergyman and speaking to a child of sin.

"Sister Prudence," said he, earnestly, "I rejoice that a merciful Providence hath turned your steps homeward, in time for me to bid you a last farewell. In a few weeks, sister, I am to sail as a missionary to the far islands of the Pacific. There is not one of these beloved faces that I shall ever hope to behold again on this earth. Oh, may I see all of them—yours and all— beyond the grave!"

A shadow flitted across the girl's countenance.

"The grave is very dark, brother," answered she, withdrawing her hand somewhat hastily from his grasp. "You must look your last at me by the light of this fire."

While this was passing, the twin girl—the rosebud that had grown on the same stem with the castaway—stood gazing at her sister, longing to fling herself upon her bosom, so that the tendrils of their hearts might intertwine again. At first she was restrained by mingled grief and shame, and by a dread that Prudence was too much changed to respond to her affection, or that her own purity would be felt as a reproach by the lost one. But, as she listened to the familiar voice, while the face grew more and more familiar, she forgot everything save that Prudence had come back. Springing forward, she would have clasped her in a close embrace. At that very instant, however, Prudence started from her chair, and held out both her hands, with a warning gesture.

"No, Mary,—no, my sister," cried she, "do not you touch me. Your bosom must not be pressed to mine!"

Mary shuddered and stood still, for she felt that something darker than the grave was between Prudence and herself, though they seemed so near each other in the light of their father's hearth, where they had grown up together. Meanwhile Prudence threw her eyes around the room, in search of one who had not yet bidden her welcome. He had withdrawn from his seat by the fireside, and was standing near the door, with his face averted so that his features could be discerned only by the flickering shadow of the profile upon the wall. But Prudence called to him, in a cheerful and kindly tone:—

"Come, Robert," said she, "won't you shake hands with your old friend?"

Robert Moore held back for a moment, but affection struggled powerfully, and overcame his pride and resentment; he rushed towards Prudence, seized her hand, and pressed it to his bosom.

"There, there, Robert," said she, smiling sadly, as she withdrew her hand, "you must not give me too warm a welcome."

And now, having exchanged greetings with each member of the family, Prudence again seated herself in the chair at John Inglefield's right hand. She was naturally a girl of quick and tender sensibilities, gladsome in her general mood, but with a bewitching pathos interfused among her merriest words and deeds. It was remarked of her, too, that she had a faculty, even from childhood, of throwing her own feelings like a spell over her companions. Such as she had been in her days of innocence, so did she appear this evening. Her friends, in the surprise and bewilderment of her return, almost forgot that she had ever left them, or that she had forfeited any of her claims to their affection. In the morning, perhaps, they might have looked at her with altered eyes, but by the Thanksgiving fireside they felt only that their own Prudence had come back to them, and were thankful. John Inglefield's rough visage brightened with the glow of his heart, as it grew warm and merry within him; once or twice, even, he laughed till the room rang again, yet seemed startled by the echo of his own mirth. The brave young minister became as frolicsome as a schoolboy. Mary, too, the rosebud, forgot that her twin-blossom had ever been torn from the stem and trampled in the dust. And as for Robert Moore, he gazed at Prudence with the bashful earnestness of love new-born, while she, with maiden coquetry, half smiled upon and half discouraged him.

In short, it was one of those intervals when sorrow vanishes in its own depth of shadow, and joy starts forth in transitory brightness. When the clock struck eight, Prudence poured out her father's customary draught of herb tea, which had been steeping by the fireside ever since twilight.

"God bless you, child," said John Inglefield, as he took the cup from her hand; "you have made your old father happy again. But we miss your mother sadly, Prudence, sadly. It seems as if she ought to be here now."

"Now, father, or never," replied Prudence.

It was now the hour for domestic worship. But while the family were making preparations for this duty, they suddenly perceived that Prudence had put on her cloak and hood, and was lifting the latch of the door.

"Prudence, Prudence! Where are you going?" cried they all with one voice.

As Prudence passed out of the door, she turned towards them, and flung back her hand with a gesture of farewell. But her face was so changed that they hardly recognized it. Sin and evil passions glowed through its comeliness, and wrought a horrible deformity; a smile gleamed in her eyes, as of triumphant mockery, at their surprise and grief.

"Daughter," cried John Inglefield, between wrath and sorrow, "stay and be your father's blessing, or take his curse with you!"

For an instant Prudence lingered and looked back into the fire- lighted room, while her countenance wore almost the expression as if she were struggling with a fiend, who had power to seize his victim even within the hallowed precincts of her father's hearth. The fiend prevailed; and Prudence vanished into the outer darkness. When the family rushed to the door, they could see nothing, but heard the sound of wheels rattling over the frozen ground.

That same night, among the painted beauties at the theatre of a neighboring city, there was one whose dissolute mirth seemed inconsistent with any sympathy for pure affections, and for the joys and griefs which are hallowed by them. Yet this was Prudence Inglefield. Her visit to the Thanksgiving fireside was the realization of one of those waking dreams in which the guilty soul will sometimes stray back to its innocence. But Sin, alas! is careful of her bond-slaves; they hear her voice, perhaps, at the holiest moment, and are constrained to go whither she summons them. The same dark power that drew Prudence Inglefield from her father's hearth—the same in its nature, though heightened then to a dread necessity—would snatch a guilty soul from the gate of heaven, and make its sin and punishment alike eternal.

—*Nathaniel Hawthorne (1804-1864)*

Two Thanksgiving Day Gentlemen

There is one day that is ours. There is one day when all we Americans who are not self-made go back to the old home to eat saleratus biscuits and marvel how much nearer to the porch the old pump looks than it used to. Bless the day. President [Theodore] Roosevelt gives it to us. We hear some talk of the Puritans, but don't just remember who they were. Bet we can lick 'em, anyhow, if they try to land again. Plymouth Rocks? Well, that sounds more familiar. Lots of us have had to come down to hens since the Turkey Trust got its work in. But somebody in Washington is leaking out advance information to 'em about these Thanksgiving proclamations.

The big city east of the cranberry bogs has made Thanksgiving Day an institution. The last Thursday in November is the only day in the year on which it recognizes the part of America lying across the ferries. It is the one day that is purely American. Yes, a day of celebration, exclusively American.

And now for the story which is to prove to you that we have traditions on this side of the ocean that are becoming older at a much rapider rate than those of England are—thanks to our git-up and enterprise.

Stuffy Pete took his seat on the third bench to the right as you enter Union Square from the east, at the walk opposite the fountain. Every Thanksgiving Day for nine years he had taken his seat there promptly at one o'clock. For every time he had done so things had happened to him— Charles Dickensy things that swelled his waistcoat above his heart, and equally on the other side.

But to-day Stuffy Pete's appearance at the annual trysting place seemed to have been rather the result of habit than of the yearly hunger which, as the philanthropists seem to think, afflicts the poor at such extended intervals.

Certainly Pete was not hungry. He had just come from a feast that had left him of his powers barely those of respiration and locomotion. His eyes were like two pale gooseberries firmly imbedded in a swollen and gravy-smeared mask of putty. His breath came in short wheezes; a senatorial roll of adipose tissue denied a fashionable set to his upturned coat collar. Buttons that had been sewed upon his clothes by kind Salvation fingers a week before flew like pop-corn, strewing the earth around him. Ragged he was, with a split shirt front open to the wishbone; but the November breeze, carrying fine snowflakes, brought him only a grateful coolness. For Stuffy Pete was overcharged with the caloric produced by a super-bountiful dinner, beginning with oysters and ending with plum pudding, and including (it seemed to him) all the roast turkey and baked potatoes and chicken salad and squash pie and ice cream in the world. Wherefore he sat, gorged, and gazed upon the world with after-dinner contempt.

The meal had been an unexpected one. He was passing a red brick mansion near the beginning of Fifth Avenue, in which lived two old ladies of ancient family and a reverence for traditions. They even denied the existence of New York, and believed that Thanksgiving Day was declared solely for Washington Square. One of their traditional habits was to station a servant at the postern gate with orders to admit the first hungry wayfarer that came along after the hour of noon had struck, and banquet him to a finish. Stuffy Pete happened to pass by on his way to the park, and the seneschal gathered him in and upheld the custom of the castle.

After Stuffy Pete had gazed straight before him for ten minutes he was conscious of a desire for a more varied field of vision. With a tremendous effort he moved his head slowly to the left, and then his eyes bulged out fearfully, and his breath ceased, and the rough-shod ends of his short legs wriggled and rustled on the gravel.

For the Old Gentleman was coming across Fourth Avenue toward his bench.

Every Thanksgiving Day for nine years the Old Gentleman had come there and found Stuffy Pete on his bench. That was a thing that the Old Gentleman was trying to make a tradition of. Every Thanksgiving Day for nine years he had found Stuffy there, and had led him to a restaurant and watched him eat a big dinner. They do those things in England unconsciously. But this is a young country, and nine years is not so bad. The Old Gentleman was a staunch American patriot, and considered himself a pioneer in American tradition. In order to become picturesque we must keep on doing one thing for a long time without ever letting it get away from us. Something like collecting the weekly dimes in industrial insurance. Or cleaning the streets.

The Old Gentleman moved, straight and stately, toward the Institution that he was rearing. Truly, the annual feeding of Stuffy Pete was nothing national in its character, such as the Magna Charta or jam for breakfast was in England. But it was a step. It was almost feudal. It showed, at least, that a Custom was not impossible to New Y—ahem!—America.

The Old Gentleman was thin and tall and sixty. He was dressed all in black, and wore the old-fashioned kind of glasses that won't stay on your nose. His hair was whiter and thinner than it had been last year, and he seemed to make more use of his big knobby cane with the crooked handle.

As his established benefactor came up, Stuffy wheezed and shuddered like some woman's over-fat pug when a street dog bristles up at him. He would have flown, but all the skill of Santos-Dumont could not have separated him from his bench. Well had the myrmidons of the two old ladies done their work.

"Good morning," said the Old Gentleman. "I am glad to perceive that the vicissitudes of another year had spared you to move in health about the beautiful world. For that blessing alone this day of thanksgiving is well proclaimed to each of us. If you will come with me, my man, I will provide you with a dinner that should make your physical being accord with the mental."

That is what the Old Gentleman said every time. Every Thanksgiving Day for nine years. The words themselves almost formed an Institution. Nothing could be compared with them except the Declaration of Independence. Always before they had been music to Stuffy's ears. But now he looked up at the Old Gentleman's face with tearful agony in his own. The fine snow almost sizzled when it fell upon his perspiring brow. But the Old Gentleman shivered a little and turned his back to the wind.

Stuffy had always wondered why the Old Gentleman spoke his speech rather sadly. He did not know that it was because he was wishing every time that he had a son to succeed him. A son who would come there after he was gone—a son who would stand proud and strong before some subsequent Stuffy and say: "In memory of my father." Then it would be an Institution.

But the Old Gentleman had no relatives. He lived in rented rooms in one of the decayed old family brownstone mansions in one of the quiet streets east of the park. In the winter he raised fuchsias in a little conservatory the size of a steamer trunk. In the spring he walked in the Easter parade. In the summer he lived at a farmhouse in the New Jersey hills, and sat in a wicker armchair, speaking of a butterfly, the ornithoptera amphrisius, that he hoped to find some day. In the autumn he fed Stuffy a dinner. These were the Old Gentleman's occupations.

Stuffy Pete looked up at him for a half minute, stewing and helpless in his own self-pity. The Old Gentleman's eyes were bright with the giving-pleasure. His face was getting more lined each year, but his little black necktie was in as jaunty a bow as ever, and his linen was beautiful and white, and his gray mustache was curled gracefully at the ends. And then Stuffy made a noise that sounded like peas bubbling in a pot. Speech was intended; and as the Old Gentleman had heard the sounds nine times before, he rightly construed them into Stuffy's old formula of acceptance.

"Thankee, sir. I'll go with ye, and much obliged. I'm very hungry, sir."

The coma of repletion had not prevented from entering Stuffy's mind the conviction that he was the basis of an Institution. His Thanksgiving appetite was not his own; it belonged by all the sacred rights of established custom, if not by the actual Statute of Limitations to this kind old gentleman, who had preempted it. True, America is free; but in order to establish tradition some one must be a repetend—a repeating decimal. The heroes are not all heroes of steel and gold. See one here that wielded only weapons of iron, badly silvered, and tin.

The Old Gentleman led his annual protégé southward to the restaurant, and to the table where the feast had always occurred. They were recognized.

"Here comes de old guy," said a waiter, "dat blows dat same bum to a meal every Thanksgiving."

The Old Gentleman sat across the table glowing like a smoked pearl at his corner-stone of future ancient Tradition. The waiters heaped the table with holiday food—and Stuffy, with a sigh that was mistaken for hunger's expression, raised knife and fork and carved for himself a crown of imperishable bay.

No more valiant hero ever fought his way through the ranks of an enemy. Turkey, chops, soups, vegetables, pies, disappeared before him as fast as they could be served. Gorged nearly to the uttermost when he entered the restaurant, the smell of food had almost caused him to lose his honor as a gentleman, but he rallied like a true knight. He saw the look of beneficent happiness on the Old Gentleman's face—a happier look than even the fuchsias and the ornithoptera amphrisius had ever brought to it—and he had not the heart to see it wane.

In an hour Stuffy leaned back with a battle won.

"Thankee kindly, sir," he puffed like leaky steam pipe; "thankee kindly for a hearty meal."

Then he arose heavily with glazed eyes and started toward the kitchen. A waiter turned him about like a top, and pointed him toward the door. The Old Gentleman carefully counted out $1.30 in silver change, leaving three nickels for the waiter.

They parted as they did each year at the door, the Old Gentleman going south, Stuffy north.

Around the first corner Stuffy turned, and stood for one minute. Then he seemed to puff out his rags as an owl puffs out his feathers, and fell to the sidewalk like a sunstricken horse.

When the ambulance came the young surgeon and the driver cursed softly at his weight. There was no smell of whiskey to justify a transfer to the patrol wagon, so Stuffy and his two dinners went to the hospital. There they stretched him on a bed and began to test him for strange diseases, with the hope of getting a chance at some problem with the bare steel.

And lo! an hour later another ambulance brought the Old Gentleman.

And they laid him on another bed and spoke of appendicitis, for he looked good for the bill.

But pretty soon one of the young doctors met one of the young nurses whose eyes he liked, and stopped to chat with her about the cases.

"That nice old gentleman over there, now," he said, "you wouldn't think that was a case of almost starvation. Proud old family, I guess. He told me he hadn't eaten a thing for three days."

—*William Sidney Porter (O. Henry) (1862-1910)*

(Picture collection, the Branch Libraries, the New York Public Library)

from
The Old New England Thanksgiving

The king and high priest of all festivals was the autumn Thanksgiving. When the apples were all gathered and the cider was all made, and the yellow pumpkins were rolled in from many a hill in billows of gold, and the corn was husked, and the labors of the season were done, and the warm, late days of Indian Summer came in, dreamy, and calm, and still, with just enough frost to crisp the ground of a morning, but with warm traces of benignant, sunny hours at noon, there came over the community a sort of genial respose of spirit —a sense of something accomplished, and of a new golden mark made in advance —and the deacon began to say to the minister, of a Sunday, "I suppose it's about time for the Thanksgiving proclamation."

—*Harriet Beecher Stowe (1811-1896)*

The Twilight of Thanksgiving

The day has lengthened into eve,
And over all the meadows
The Twilight's silent shuttles weave
Their sombre web of shadows;
With northern lights the cloudless skies
Are faintly phosphorescent,
And just above yon wooded rise
The new moon shows her crescent.

Before the evening lamps are lit,
While day and night commingle,
The sire and matron come and sit
Beside the cozy ingle;
And softly speak of the delight
Within their bosoms swelling,
Because beneath their roof to-night
Their dear ones all are dwelling.

And when around the cheerful blaze
The young folks take their places,
What blissful dreams of other days
Light up their aged faces!
The past returns with all its joys,
And they again are living
The years in which, as girls and boys,
Their children kept Thanksgiving.

The stalwart son recalls the time
When, urged to the endeavor,
He tried the well-greased pole to climb,
And failed of fame forever.
The daughter tells of her emprise
When, as a new beginner,

She helped her mother make the pies
For the Thanksgiving dinner.

And thus with laugh and jest and song,
And tender recollections,
Love speeds the happy hours along,
And fosters fond affections;
While Fancy, listening to the mirth,
And dreaming pleasant fictions,
Imagines through the winds on earth
That heaven breathes benedictions.
—*William D. Kelley (1814-1890)*

Selection

Heap high the farmer's wintry hoard!
Heap high the golden corn!
No richer gift has Autumn poured
From out her lavish horn.

Let other lands exulting glean
The apple from the pine,
The orange from its glossy green,
The cluster from the vine.

But let the good old corn adorn,
The hills our fathers trod;
Still let us for His golden corn,
Send up our thanks to God.
—*John Greenleaf Whittier (1807-1892)*

The Thanksgiving in Boston Harbor

"Praise ye the Lord!" The psalm to-day
Still rises on our ears,
Borne from the hills of Boston Bay
Through five times fifty years,
When Winthrop's fleet from Yarmouth crept
Out to the open main,
And through the widening waters swept,
In April sun and rain.
"Pray to the Lord with fervent lips,"
The leader shouted, "pray;"
And prayer arose from all the ships
As faded Yarmouth Bay.

They passed the Scilly Isles that day,
And May-days came, and June,
And thrice upon the ocean lay
The full orb of the moon.
And as that day, on Yarmouth Bay,
Ere England sunk from view,
While yet the rippling Solent lay
In April skies of blue,
"Pray to the Lord with fervent lips,"
Each morn was shouted, "pray;"
And prayer arose from all the ships,
As first in Yarmouth Bay.

Blew warm the breeze o'er Western seas,
Through Maytime morns, and June,
Till hailed these souls the Isles of Shoals,
Low 'neath the summer moon;
And as Cape Ann arose to view,
And Norman's Woe they passed,

The wood-doves came the white mists through,
And circled round each mast.
"Pray to the Lord with fervent lips,"
Then called the leader, "pray;"
And prayer arose from all the ships,
As first in Yarmouth Bay.

Above the sea the hill-tops fair—
God's towers—began to rise,
And odors rare breathe through the air,
Like balms of Paradise.
Through burning skies the ospreys flew,
And near the pine-cooled shores
Danced airy boat and thin canoe,
To flash of sunlit oars.
"Pray to the Lord with fervent lips,"
The leader shouted, "pray!"
Then prayer arose, and all the ships
Sailed into Boston Bay.

The white wings folded, anchors down,
The sea-worn fleet in line,
Fair rose the hills where Boston Town
Should rise from clouds of pine;
Fair was the harbor, summit-walled,
And placid lay the sea.
"Praise ye the Lord," the leader called;
"Praise ye the Lord," spake he.
"Give thanks to God with fervent lips,
Give thanks to God to-day,"
The anthem rose from all the ships
Safe moored in Boston Bay.

Our fathers' prayers have changed to psalms,
As David's treasures old
Turned, on the Temple's giant arms,

To lily-work of gold.
Ho! vanished ships from Yarmouth's tide,
Ho! ships of Boston Bay,
Your prayers have crossed the centuries wide
To this Thanksgiving Day!
We pray to God with fervent lips,
We praise the Lord to-day,
As prayers arose from Yarmouth ships,
But psalms from Boston Bay.
—*Hezekiah Butterworth (1839-1905)*

A Rhyme for Thanksgiving Day

I count up in this hour of cheer
The blessings of a busy year:

A roof so low I lost no strain,
No ripple of the friendly rain,

A chimney where all Winter long
The logs give back the wild bird's song.

The tree-toad that is the first to cheer
With crinkling flute the green o' the year

The cricket on the garden mount,
Stitching the dark with threads of sound.

The wind that cools my hidden spring
And sets my corn-field whispering,

And shakes with Autumn breath for me
Late apples from the apple-tree.

The shy paths darting thru the wheat,
Marked by the prints of little feet—

Gray squirrels on their thrifty round,
Grows condescending to the ground.

That leafy hollow that was stirred
A hundred mornings by a bird

Which sang at daybreak on a brier,
Setting the gray of dawn afire!

The lone star and the shadowed hush
That comes at evening, when the thrush

Turns with his wild heart all the long
Soft twilight to a mystic song.

The tender sorrow, too, that came
To leave me nevermore the same;

The love and memories and the wilde
Light laughter of a little child.

And deep thanksgiving for the friend
Who came when all things seemed to end;

Whose courage helped me lift the load,
Whose spirit lit the darkened road.
  —*Edwin Markham (1852-1940)*

We Thank Thee

For flowers that bloom about our feet;
For tender grass, so fresh, so sweet;
For song of bird, and hum of bee;
For all Things fair we hear or see,
    Father in heaven, we thank Thee!

For blue of stream and blue of sky;
For pleasant shade of branches high;
For fragrant air and cooling breeze;
For beauty of the blooming trees,
    Father in heaven, we thank Thee!
—*Ralph Waldo Emerson (1803-1882)*

AFTER-DINNER GAMES

"It is a happy talent
to know how to play."
—Ralph Waldo Emerson, *Journals,* 1834

"Thanksgiving Games," nineteenth century, artist unknown (Picture collection, the Branch Libraries, the New York Public Library)

The spirit of Thanksgiving has a way of making people want to have fun together. And what better way to have fun together than to play games? Games of all sorts have been played on Thanksgiving Day for as long as there has been a Thanksgiving. The earliest Thanksgivings featured turkey shoots and sporting events, and today we continue that first tradition with games of our own.

The five group games described here all have a long tradition. Many became popular during the late 1800s when after-dinner entertainment depended upon the wit and ingenuity of the partygoers, and not on radio or television. Some games, like "Charades," probably date back hundreds of years, while others, like the psychological game "Essence" or the word game "Dictionary," are comparatively more recent. All of them are perfect for adults and children alike.

In these days of mass entertainment, you might encounter a little natural resistance to acting out the name of your favorite movie or repeating the phrase "Marla likes milk. Do you like milk as much?" in someone's ear during a game of "Telephone." But don't worry. It won't take but a moment's hesitation before even the most reluctant guest is completely involved. This year, once the leftovers have been stored and the dishes put away, keep the spirit of togetherness going and rediscover the pleasure of an old-fashioned Thanksgiving evening, filled with fun and games.

(Picture collection, the Branch Libraries, the New York Public Library)

Charades

PLAYERS:
Four or more. Can be played individually, in pairs or in teams.

OBJECT:
To act out—without speaking—a familiar name, title, or phrase that can be guessed quickly by your teammates.

DIRECTIONS:
The players agree mutually on a general topic or topics from which names or titles or phrases may be chosen. Books, films, plays, celebrities, and clichés are popular subjects. Each team then chooses a timekeeper. If books, for example, are the topic, each player chooses a number of titles that will be difficult for the others to act out in pantomime and writes each title on a separate piece of paper, folding the paper afterward, and adding the papers to a pile from which opponents can choose. One player chooses a paper from an opponent's selection and acts out the title (word for word) without speaking to his team. When the correct title is guessed, the timekeeper records the amount of time elapsed. The same follows for the other team. There is usually a three-minute limit per title for each team. There is no limit to the number of rounds played. The winner at the end of the game is the team with the lowest recorded time.

TIPS:
- Choose material that will be difficult to act out in pantomime.
- Common hand movements for general information:
     Cranking a projector = Movie
     Opening hands palms up at reading distance = Book
     Parting stage curtains = Play
     Making box in front of face with hands = Television
     Showing number on fingers = Number of words in phrase
     Showing number on fingers = Number of syllables in word
     Pulling ear lobe = Sounds like
     Pointing to eyes = Looks like

Dictionary

PLAYERS:
Any number.

OBJECT:
To guess the correct meaning of an unfamiliar word.

DIRECTIONS:
One player chooses a word from the dictionary, calls it out, and spells it aloud, and verifies (as best possible) that it is unknown to all other players. On identical pieces of paper, the other players write down what they believe are plausible definitions. The person reading the definition also writes the correct definition on a piece of paper. All definitions are put into a container, such as a hat, and then picked out and read by the selector. The other players vote once on which definition is correct. The player who chooses the correct definition is awarded a point. If no one chooses the correct definition, the player who chose the word in question receives bonus points. Players who wrote bogus definitions receive a point for every player who chose their definition.

TIPS:
- For variety, use an old, large dictionary.
- Choose words that are archaic, odd, or difficult to break down into Latin roots.

(Picture collection, the Branch Libraries, the New York Public Library)

Telephone

PLAYERS:
Six or more.

OBJECT:
To deliver a short message correctly to all players.

DIRECTIONS:
Players arrange themselves in a circle. One player is designated as "message giver," and whispers a sentence to the player on his or her immediate right. The message may not be repeated or written down. That player whispers the message to the next player on the right. This sequence continues until all players have received and transmitted the message. When it has come full circle, the last player announces the message. The message giver then announces the original sentence: it seldom bears any resemblance to the final version.

TIPS:
- Keep the original message simple; this is not a test of the ability to create long and complicated sentences.
- Try to choose sentences that will be humorous if altered slightly, such as "Peter Piper picked a peck of pickled peppers."

(Picture collection, the Branch Libraries, the New York Public Library)

Twenty Questions

PLAYERS:
Two or more.

OBJECT:
To determine the identity of an unknown subject by asking as few questions as possible.

DIRECTIONS:
The players agree on a range of categories, such as animal, vegetable, and mineral. One player secretly decides on an object, person, or idea that fits into one of those categories, such as "apple." The other players take turns asking questions to determine the identity of that subject. The questions must be able to be answered simply, either with yes or no, or a few words. Long, descriptive answers are not permitted. Only twenty questions may be asked. The winner is either the player who identifies the unknown subject or the person whose choice of subject stumps the others.

TIPS:
- The subject to be guessed can be limited to the areas of animal, vegetable, or mineral, but they are not the only categories possible. Periods of history, names of celebrities, and state capitals are other possibilities.
- Ask leading questions that will narrow your choices as much as possible.

"[Thanksgiving] as founded be th' Puritans to give thanks f'r bein' presarved fr'm th' Indyans, an' we keep it to give thanks we are presarved fr'm th' Puritans."
—Finley Peter Dunne, "Thanksgiving," *Mr. Dooley's Opinions, 1901*

Essence

PLAYERS:
Five or more.

OBJECT:
To determine the identity of the person being discussed from answers given about him or her.

DIRECTIONS:
One player leaves the room while the rest of the group decides on the player who is to be described in the round. The player who left the room returns and asks three questions to determine the identity of that person. The questions must follow the following model: ''What kind of car (or any other object or action) does this person remind you of?'' All of the players, including the player who is being discussed, must answer each question. At the end of the questioning, the person tries to guess the correct identity.

TIPS:
- Common types for questions include animal, fruit, vegetable, car, flower.
- Keep types general, so that there may be a wide range of answers.

(Picture collection, the Branch Libraries,
the New York Public Library)

CHAP 6 TER

THANKSGIVING SING-ALONGS

*"And the night shall be
filled with music—"*

—Henry Wadsworth Longfellow, "The Day Is Done," 1844

"Thanksgiving Songs in the Parlor," nineteenth century, artist unknown (Culver Pictures)

N o Thanksgiving Day is complete without song. Whether you're standing around the piano singing old melodies, strumming on a guitar you take out of the closet once a year, or singing in the kitchen, making up your own verses as you go, singing has a way of making each person a part of the family and reminding us of the reasons we celebrate: love, companionship, and gratitude for the pleasures of life.

In the earliest days of the Thanksgiving holiday, psalms put to music brought to life the spiritual overtones of the religious feast. As Thanksgiving became more of a general holiday that stressed patriotism and family reunions, as well as giving thanks, the choice of newer songs reflected the change. Songs like "Turkey in the Straw" and "Over the River and Through the Wood" became popular in the 1800s and are holiday standards today. Hymns of thanksgiving, such as "Come, Ye Thankful People, Come," or "Prayer of Thanksgiving," are now standards for holiday religious services.

The six songs in this section reflect the range of celebration found in Thanksgiving. Some are pious, some reverent, some rousing. All are fun. Make singing together at Thanksgiving an annual event, and bring joy to your house as you raise your voices in song together.

Over the River and Through the Wood

This rollicking tune has been a holiday favorite for over a century. The lyrics were originally published as a poem called "Thanksgiving Day."

Lydia Maria Child   Traditional (U.S.)

2. Over the river and through the wood and straight to the barnyard gate,
We seem to go so very slow, and it's so hard to wait,
Over the river and through the wood, now grandmother's cap I spy.
Hurrah for the fun, the pudding's done, hurrah for the pumkin pie.

3. Over the river and through the wood, now soon we'll be on our way,
There's feasting and fun for every one, for this is Thanksgiving day,
Over the river and through the wood, get on, my dapple grey,
The woods will ring with songs we sing, for this is Thanksgiving day.

Turkey in the Straw

This Thanksgiving Day favorite, which has at least a thousand verses in all its variations, is an ideal stimulant for square dancing or group singing.

Introduction

Traditional (U.S.)

1. Went — out to milk and I did - n't know how, I —
milked the goat — in - stead of the cow, Saw a
tur - key strut on a pile of straw while a - wink - ing at his —

moth - er - in - law. Turkey in the straw,

Chorus

Straw! Straw! Tur-key in the hay, Hay! Hay!

Roll 'em up and twist 'em up a high tuck a haw, And we'll

play a lit - tle tune__ called the "Tur-key in the Straw"

2. Well, that old bird had a wooden leg,
The best old turkey that ever laid an egg.
He laid more eggs than the hens on the farm;
Thought that laying those eggs would do no harm.

Chorus

Come, Ye Thankful People, Come

The English composer Sir George J. Elvey, who wrote the music to this hymn, probably in 1844, was the organist at St. George's Chapel, Windsor Castle, for nearly fifty years, and was knighted by Queen Victoria. The lyrics were written by Henry Alford.

Henry Alford (1810-1871)
altered by **Hugh Hartshorne**

George J. Elvey (1816-1893)

1. Come ye thank-ful peo - ple, come, Raise the song of har - vest home; All is safe-ly gath - ered in, Ere the win - ter storms be - gin; God, our Mak - er, doth pro - vide For our wants to be sup - plied; Come to God's own tem - ple, come, Raise the song of har - vest home

2. All the world is God's own field, Fruit unto his praise to yield;
Wheat and tares together sown, Unto joy or sorrow grown:
Frist the blade, and then the ear, Then the full corn shall appear:
Grant, O harvest Lord, that we Wholesome grain and pure may be.

3. For the Lord our God shall come, And shall take his harvest home;
From his field shall in that day All offences purge away;
Give his angels charge at last In the fire the tares to cast,
But the fruitful ears to store In his garner evermore.

4. Even so, Lord, quickly come To thy final harvest-home;
Gather thou thy people in, Free from sorrow, free from sin;
There, for ever purified, In thy presence to abide:
Come, with all thine angels, come, Raise the glorious harvest-home.

On the First Thanksgiving Day

This simple hymn of gratitude is an American folk standard.

Traditional (U.S.)

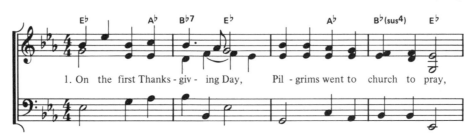

1. On the first Thanks - giv - ing Day, Pil - grims went to church to pray,

Thanked the Lord for sun and rain, Thanked him for the fields of grain.

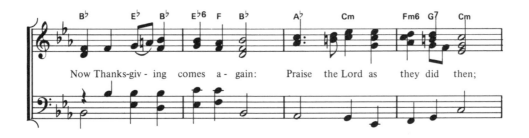

Now Thanks-giv - ing comes a - gain: Praise the Lord as they did then;

Thank him for the sun and rain, Thank him for the fields of grain.

2. On the first Thanksgiving Day, Pilgrim bowed their heads to pray.
Thanked the Lord for food to share, Thanked him for a day os fair.
Now Thanksgiving comes again: Praise the Lord as they did then;
Thank him for our food to share, Thank him for a day so fair.

Prayer of Thanksgiving
(We Gather Together)

In the early 1600s, the Dutch settlers brought this prayer to the New World. Music was added and it became a favorite in the colonies. The colony, originally called New Netherland, included the coastal areas that later became New York, New Jersey, and Delaware.

Anonymous
Translated by
Theodore Baker (1851-1934)

Traditional (Netherlands)

2. Beside us to guide us, our God with us joining,
   Ordaining, maintaining his kingdom divine;
   So from the beginning the fight we were winning:
   Thou, Lord, wast at our side: all glory be thine!

3. We all do extol thee, thou leader triumphant,
   And pray that thou still our defender wilt be.
   Let thy congregation escape tribulation:
   Thy Name be ever praised! O Lord, make us free!

Amazing Grace

This classic hymn, written at the turn of the nineteenth century by John Newton, can easily be adapted to any size group or to any instrumental accompaniment.

John Newton (1727-1807)   Traditional (U.S.)

2. 'Twas grace that taught my heart to fear, And grace that fear relieved.
How precious did that grace appear   The hour I first believed.

3. Through many dangers, toils, and snares   We have already come;
'Twas grace that led us safe thus far,   And grace will lead us home.

4. The Lord has promised good to me,   His word my hope secures;
He will my shield and portion be   As long as life endures.

5. When we've been here ten thousand years,   Bright shining as the sun,
We've no less days to sing God's praise   Than when we first begun.

Our Thanksgiving Memories

DATE: _____

PLACE: _____

GUESTS:

_____   _____
_____   _____
_____   _____
_____   _____
_____   _____
_____   _____
_____   _____

TURKEY CARVER: _____

THANKSGIVING MENU:

_____   _____
_____   _____
_____   _____
_____   _____
_____   _____
_____   _____
_____   _____

SPECIAL MEMORIES: _____

_____
_____
_____
_____
_____
_____
_____
_____

Our Thanksgiving Memories

DATE: _____

PLACE: _____

GUESTS:

_____   _____
_____   _____
_____   _____
_____   _____
_____   _____
_____   _____
_____   _____
_____   _____

TURKEY CARVER: _____

THANKSGIVING MENU:

_____   _____
_____   _____
_____   _____
_____   _____
_____   _____
_____   _____
_____   _____

SPECIAL MEMORIES: _____

_____
_____
_____
_____
_____
_____
_____

Our Thanksgiving Memories

DATE: _____

PLACE: _____

GUESTS:

_____   _____
_____   _____
_____   _____
_____   _____
_____   _____
_____   _____
_____   _____

TURKEY CARVER: _____

THANKSGIVING MENU:

_____   _____
_____   _____
_____   _____
_____   _____
_____   _____
_____   _____

SPECIAL MEMORIES: _____

_____
_____
_____
_____
_____
_____
_____

Our Thanksgiving Memories

DATE: _____

PLACE: _____

GUESTS:

_____   _____
_____   _____
_____   _____
_____   _____
_____   _____
_____   _____
_____   _____
_____   _____

TURKEY CARVER: _____

THANKSGIVING MENU:

_____   _____
_____   _____
_____   _____
_____   _____
_____   _____
_____   _____
_____   _____
_____   _____

SPECIAL MEMORIES: _____

_____
_____
_____
_____
_____
_____
_____

Our Thanksgiving Football Scorecard

DATE: _____

TEAMS: _____

STADIUM: _____

QUARTERBACKS: _____

POINT SPREAD: _____

FINAL SCORE: _____

OUTSTANDING PLAYS: _____

_____

_____

* * * * * *

DATE: _____

TEAMS: _____

STADIUM: _____

QUARTERBACKS: _____

POINT SPREAD: _____

FINAL SCORE: _____

OUTSTANDING PLAYS: _____

_____

_____

* * * * * *

DATE: _____

TEAMS: _____

STADIUM: _____

QUARTERBACKS: _____

POINT SPREAD: _____

FINAL SCORE: _____

OUTSTANDING PLAYS: _____

_____

_____

Our Thanksgiving Football Scorecard

DATE: _____

TEAMS:_____

STADIUM: _____

QUARTERBACKS:_____

POINT SPREAD:_____

FINAL SCORE: _____

OUTSTANDING PLAYS: _____

_____

_____

******

DATE: _____

TEAMS:_____

STADIUM: _____

QUARTERBACKS:_____

POINT SPREAD:_____

FINAL SCORE: _____

OUTSTANDING PLAYS: _____

_____

_____

******

DATE: _____

TEAMS:_____

STADIUM: _____

QUARTERBACKS:_____

POINT SPREAD:_____

FINAL SCORE: _____

OUTSTANDING PLAYS: _____

_____

_____

Our Thanksgiving Photo Album

FOR FURTHER INFORMATION

BOOKS

1. Appelbaum, Diana Karter. *Thanksgiving: An American Holiday, An American History.* New York: Facts on File Publications, 1984.

2. Bradford, William. *Of Plymouth Plantation: 1620-1647.* Ed. Samuel Eliot Morison. New York: Alfred A. Knopf, 1952.

3. Heath, Dwight B., ed. *Mourt's Relation: A Relation or Journal of the English Plantation settled at Plymouth in New England, by certain English adventurers both merchants and others.* New York: Corinth Books, 1963.

4. Schauffler, Robert Haven. *Thanksgiving: Its Origin, Celebration, and Significance as Related in Prose and Verse.* New York: Moffat, Yard and Co., 1907.

MUSEUMS, FOUNDATIONS, AND ASSOCIATIONS

1. Museum of the American Indian, Broadway at 155 Street, New York, NY 10032. Devoted to the collection, preservation, study, and exhibition of all things connected with the Indians of the Americas.

2. Museum of the American Indian Library, 9 Westchester Square, The Bronx, NY 10461. A leading research source on the Indians.

3. National Thanksgiving Commission, Box 1777, Dallas, TX 75221. Studies the tradition of thanksgiving in its many forms throughout the world.

4. The National Wild Turkey Federation, Wild Turkey Building, P.O. Box 530, Edgefield, SC 29824. Dedicated to protecting the wild turkey and insuring its future.

5. Old Sturbridge Village, Sturbridge, MA 01566. A "living museum" of early New England that recreates an early American Thanksgiving every November, with traditional foods.

6. Plimouth Plantation, P.O. Box 1620, Plymouth, MA 02360. This "Living Museum of 17th Century Plymouth" recreates a 1627 Pilgrim village, a Wampanoag campsite, and a ship, *Mayflower II.*

COUNTRY INNS AND HISTORIC VILLAGES
CITED IN "THE THANKSGIVING FEAST"

AMHERST SHORE COUNTRY INN
R.R. 2
Amherst, Nova Scotia B4H 3X9 CANADA
Donna Laceby, Innkeeper
(902) 667-4800

ARKANSAS TERRITORIAL RESTORATION
Corner of Third and Scott
Little Rock, AR 72201
(501) 371-2348

BENN CONGER INN
206 West Cortland Street
Groton, NY 13073
Mark Bloom, Innkeeper
(607) 898-5817

CARTER HOUSE BED AND BREAKFAST INN
1033 3rd Street
Eureka, CA 95501
Mark and Christi Carter, Innkeepers
(707) 445-1390

THE COLONIAL WILLIAMSBURG FOUNDATION
Williamsburg, VA 23185
(703) 229-1000

HANCOCK SHAKER VILLAGE
P.O. Box 898
Pittsfield, MA 01202
Amy Bess Miller, President
(413) 443-0188

INN OF THE GOLDEN OX
1360 Main Street
Route 6A and Tubman Road
Brewster, MA 02631
David and Eileen Gibson, Innkeepers
(617) 896-3111

MILLBROOK LODGE
RFD Box 62
Waitsfield, VT 05673
Joan and Thom Gorman, Innkeepers
(802) 496-2405

OLD STURBRIDGE VILLAGE
Sturbridge, MA 01566
(617) 347-3362

PATCHWORK QUILT COUNTRY INN
11748 County Road 2
Middlebury, IN 46540
Michele Lovejoy Goebel, Innkeeper
(219) 825-2417

PLIMOUTH PLANTATION
P.O. Box 1620
Plimouth, MA 02360
(617) 347-3362

SCHUMACHER'S NEW PRAGUE HOTEL
212 West Main Street
New Prague, MN 56071
Kathleen Schumacher, Innkeeper
John Schumacher, Executive Chef
(612) 758-2133

SHELTER HARBOR INN
Route One, Shelter Harbor
Westerly, RI 02891
Jim and Debbye Dey, Innkeepers
Jeffrey P. Houston, Chef
(401) 322-8883

THE SMITH HOUSE
202 South Chestatee Street
Dahlonega, GA 30533
Christie Seabolt, Manager
(404) 864-3566

WHITE CLOUD NATURAL FOODS INN
R.D. 1, Box 215
Newfoundland, PA 18445
George D. Wilkinson, Innkeeper
(717) 676-3162

(Information as of June 1987)

(Culver Pictures)